CATHOLIC SPIRITUAL PRACTICES

A TREASURY OF OLD & NEW

EDITED BY COLLEEN M. GRIFFITH
& THOMAS H. GROOME

PARACLETE PRESS
BREWSTER, MASSACHUSETTS

Catholic Spiritual Practices: A Treasury of Old and New

2012 First Printing

Copyright © 2012 by The Trustees of Boston College

ISBN 978-1-61261-246-1

Library of Congress Cataloging-in-Publication Data

Catholic spiritual practices : a treasury of old and new /
edited by Colleen M. Griffith and Thomas H. Groome.
    p. cm.
  ISBN 978-1-61261-246-1
  1. Spiritual life—Catholic Church. I. Griffith, Colleen M.
II. Groome, Thomas H.
  BX2350.3.C3825 2012
  248.4'82—dc23
                                        2012023580

10 9 8 7 6 5 4 3 2 1

Published by Paraclete Press
Brewster, Massachusetts
www.paracletepress.com
Printed in the United States of America

CONTENTS

PART ONE

PRACTICES OF PRAYER

PART TWO

PRACTICES OF CARE

PRACTICES OF SPIRITUAL GROWTH

CATHOLIC SPIRITUALITY

IN PRACTICE

Colleen M. Griffith

*S*PIRITUALITY IS A BUZZWORD in our time, one that generates much positive reception. Spiritual seekers abound, and there are myriad resources available to draw upon that bear the name "spiritual practice." Spiritual materials in bookstores and on the Internet continue to multiply at a staggering pace, as people from all walks of life and religious persuasions identify "becoming spiritual" as a primary life goal.

The term *spirituality* may carry star power here at the start of the twenty-first century, but there is much confusion about what it actually means. It is perplexing, for example, to sort through everything that presents itself as a spiritual practice. The task becomes all the more challenging when set against the backdrop of a growing popular assumption that spirituality and religion are separate entities.

Scholars in the study of spirituality raise substantial concern about the widening gulf perceived between spirituality and religious traditions. One wonders if spirituality is becoming a new commodity in this consumerist culture of ours. Sadly, it sometimes seems so. Too often, spirituality is being presented or sold as the new substitute for religion. A split between spirituality and religious tradition ensues, a split rife with dangers, and one that this book aims to address.

Spirituality and Religion

Walk across any college campus these days and you are likely to hear some version of the comment, "I'm spiritual, but not religious." The utterance usually suggests more than unfamiliarity with one's religious tradition of origin. It points often to dissatisfaction with a particular expression of a religious institution. Sometimes it signals a perception of religion as anemic and staid, as being more concerned with right beliefs than with life-orienting practices.

Claims for being "spiritual" but "not religious" deserve probing. Without doubt, religious institutions, ever human, need to engage in more substantive dialogue, self-critique, renewal, and reform. And yes, more attention must be placed on spiritual practices as central to the "content" of the faith handed down. But one can't afford to view spirituality as a substitute for religion.

A spirituality that is disconnected from religious tradition is bereft of both community and history; it has no recourse to the benefits of a larger body of discourse and practice, and it lacks accountability. Such spirituality quickly becomes privatized and rootless, something directly opposite to the Christian understanding of "life in the Spirit."

Christian Spirituality

From a Christian perspective, spirituality can be traced back to the letters of St. Paul in which he uses the Greek term *pneuma*, meaning "breath," "spirit," or "soul," to signal a life lived in alignment with God. Christian spirituality presumes, through God's grace, a human desire and capacity for growing in union with the triune God. It encompasses the dynamic character of human life lived in conscious relationship with God in Christ through the Spirit, as experienced within a community of believers. To live a Christian spirituality is to attend to what is of God and to deepen in a life of conversion that has discipleship as its goal. Christian spirituality exists in its finest expression in the living out of one's baptismal promises. At the heart of these promises stands the rejection of everything that is not of God and a decision to live in accord with the energies and ways of the triune God. Renewed commitment to our baptismal promises is made possible by God's grace, sustained by Christian community, and supported through engagement in meaningful spiritual practices.

This book seeks to present an array of Christian spiritual practices that have nurtured the lives of generations of Catholic Christians past and present. The practices included have long roots in the Catholic tradition. They have stood the test of time, demonstrating adaptability in multiple sociocultural contexts. One finds "practices of prayer," "practices of care," and "practices of growth" assembled here, as Catholic Christian spirituality has historically emphasized a strong connection between prayer and praxis and a need for development in faith. The practices included reflect a Catholic understanding of the person, a Catholic theology of revelation, and a Catholic sense of sacramentality. "Drawing from the storeroom both the old and the new" (Matt. 13:52), this collection offers readers lively entry into the shape and character of Catholic spiritual practice today.

The Nature and Purpose
of Spiritual Practice

Spiritual practices are concrete and specific. They are consciously chosen, intentional actions that give practical purpose to faith. Situated between life as we know it and life in its hoped-for fullness, spiritual practices are imbued with a sense of our relatedness to God, others, and the earth. Influencing our dispositions and outlooks on the world, spiritual practices render us more open and responsive to the dynamic activity of God's grace, and they move us toward greater spiritual maturity.

You, our reader, may have a particular concern for the practical steps involved in specific practices. In the pages that follow, you will hopefully discover that these authors directly address the "how-to" questions, making it possible for you to learn about and engage in a spiritual practice for the first time. Emphasis is put on the purpose and relevance of specific practices.

Why practice? We engage in spiritual practices because we seek a *way of life*, an embodied faith that touches us and changes us. We opt in spiritual practice for a "knowing" that springs from the heart's core, the *lev,* spoken about in the Hebrew Scriptures as the center of our affections (Ps. 4:7), the source of our reflection (Isa. 6:10), and the foundation of our will (1 Sam. 24:5).

The point of spiritual practice is never mastery, but rather deeper relational life, a kind of living that makes a rich appropriation of one's faith all the more possible.

Catholic Christianity is indeed a tradition abundant in practice. It is our hope that you will discover here a treasury of formative practices that will vivify and nurture your spiritual life. In the vast storeroom of Catholic Christian tradition, you can find all kinds of gemstones, practices to be received, lived into, and reshaped in time and place for generations to come. It is for that reason that we are here.

PART ONE

PRACTICES *of* PRAYER

THE LORD'S PRAYER

PRAYING THE OUR FATHER

N. T. Wright

SIMPLE YET PROFOUND, ancient yet always fresh; deeply Jewish yet available to all, the Lord's Prayer offers the central message of Jesus in the form best suited to its appropriation. Jesus did not come, after all, merely to teach true doctrine and ethics, but to bring about God's kingdom; within that sovereign and saving rule, human beings are caught up with the challenge and invitation to corporate and personal renewal, as deep as the human heart, as wide as the world. To pray this prayer with full attention and intention is to partake in this renewal.

The prayer occurs in Matthew 6:9–13, within the Sermon on the Mount; in Luke 11:2–4, answering the disciples' request for a prayer; and in Didache 8:2, which instructs that the prayer be used three times daily. Luke's text is shorter, with some changes in the Greek; Matthew's is the one that has become widespread in the church, with some traditions also adding Didache 10:5 ("remember, Lord, your church . . ."). The doxology ("yours is the kingdom, the power and the glory, forever") is probably not original, but became part of the prayer very early on in the life of the church. The prayer clearly stems from an Aramaic original, and it is virtually certain that it represents what Jesus taught.

The prayer is rooted, in shape and content, in older Jewish traditions. But the particular combination of elements marks it out as belonging within Jesus's aim of inaugurating God's kingdom, and his invitation to live by this kingdom in advance of its full appearing. It divides into two parts, the first (in the longer form) containing three petitions about God's purposes and glory, and the second three petitions for human need.

The address, "Our Father," expresses the intimate trust which characterizes Christian prayer. It evokes the Jewish belief that Israel, God's people, was his firstborn son (Exod. 4:22; Isa. 63:16; 64:8). The Aramaic word Abba, "Father," expresses Jesus' own intimate sense of sonship (e.g., Mk. 14:36) and the early church's sense of sharing that sonship through the Spirit (Rom. 8:16; Gal. 4:6, where the Lord's Prayer may well be in mind).

The first three petitions pray that God's glory and purpose may come to birth throughout creation. God's name is sanctified, held in honor, when his world is ruled by his wisdom and power, and his image-bearing human creatures worship him and reflect his glory in the world. His kingdom comes through Jesus's death and resurrection and his final victory over death itself (1 Cor. 15:24–28), and through every intermediate victory of his love over the powers of the world. The prayer for God's will to be done on earth as in heaven indicates, despite centuries of misunderstanding, that Christianity is not about escaping earth and going to heaven instead, but rather that God wills to renew both heaven and earth and bring them into ultimate unity (Rev. 21).

Emboldened by this trust in God and his kingdom, the last three petitions express the basic needs of those who live between Jesus's initial victory and his final triumph. Bread for today (Matthew) and every day (Luke) symbolizes our constant dependence on the creator. Forgiveness, both of sin and of material debt, is the central blessing of the new covenant (Jer. 31:34; Matt. 26:28), obtained through Jesus's death. The church here commits itself in turn to forgive (emphasized in Matt. 6:15; 18:21–35). Those who claim the new covenant blessing must live as new covenant people; the heart renewed by God's forgiveness cannot but offer forgiveness to others. The final petition for rescue from danger and evil has two branches. First, we pray to be spared the ultimate test, whether that of fierce temptation or, more specifically, the "tribulation," the "time of trial," which in early Judaism was believed to be coming upon the world (compare Matt. 26:41, where it seems that Jesus will face this "tribulation" alone). Then we pray to be delivered both from evil in general and from "the evil one"; the original wording could be taken either way, and both may be in view.

From very early, the Lord's Prayer has been at the center of Christian devotion and liturgy, not least at the Eucharist. Most of the great spiritual writers have expounded it and drawn on it. Alongside its regular use as a straightforward prayer, some have employed it as a framework, allowing other concerns to cluster around its various petitions. Others have used it, like the "Jesus prayer," as a steady, rhythmic subterranean flow, beneath the bustle of ordinary life. It is, above all, a prayer which unites Christians of every background and tradition. It could energize and sustain fresh growth in shared ecumenical witness and life.

All: Our Father, who art in heaven, hallowed be thy name;

thy kingdom come;

thy will be done on earth as it is in heaven.

Give us this day our daily bread;

and forgive us our trespasses as we forgive those who

trespass against us;

and lead us not into temptation, but deliver us from evil.

Priest: Deliver us, Lord, from every evil, and grant us peace in

our day. In your mercy keep us free from sin and protect

us from all anxiety as we wait in joyful hope for the

coming of our Savior, Jesus Christ.

All: For the kingdom, the power, and the glory are yours, now

and forever.

PRAYING WITH THE SAINTS

PRACTICES OF HOPEFUL REMEMBRANCE

Elizabeth A. Johnson, CSJ

I N ITS PLENITUDE, the symbol of the communion of saints signifies that those who seek the face of the living God today belong to a great historical company, an intergenerational band of the friends of God and prophets that includes the living and the dead, joined in community with the cosmic world, all connected in the gracious, compassionate love of Holy Wisdom who, in the midst of historical struggle, sin, and defeat, continuously renews her gift of saving, healing grace. How does this doctrinal symbol appear concretely in prayer and piety to nourish the vitality of the *ekklesia*? One fire kindles another—but how are the sparks to fly? What practices can release the liberating power of the heritage of all saints to stir the affections and motivate action?

Under the traditional patronage model of the saints, a vast set of devotions grew up known collectively as the *cultus sanctorum*, or cult of the saints. Living persons established relations with the holy ones in heaven in numerous ways such as pilgrimages, novenas, veneration of relics, the use of medals, and many other devotional practices designed to facilitate protection and help in the trials of life. It is this pattern of veneration that has so diminished in postconciliar, postcritical culture, with its realignment of the Counter-Reformation religious paradigm on the one hand and its anonymous social pressures that destroy society's feeling of community with the dead on the other. But as Scripture and the early age of the martyrs show, a patronage model is not the only possibility available for the practice of the communion of saints. A companionship model calls forth its own concrete expressions, many still in the process of being shaped in the current age as different groups devise forms of keeping memory.

"Remembering the dead," writes theologian Karl Rahner, "becomes a prayer even if it does not contain a specific petition to the 'saints,' a plea for their intercession," for it ultimately leads the mind and heart into the mystery of God. In modern and postmodern culture, such prayer through acts of remembrance and hope awakens consciousness and revitalizes the spirit. It contributes to building the church into a living community of memory and hope with "habits of the heart" that make the life of discipleship an attractive option. In its cultural setting, hopeful remembrance in fact is an act of resistance to banality, to debasement of persons and the earth, to consumerism, to individual isolation, to personal drift and apathy, to hopelessness and resignation.

Prayer of Praise and Lament in a Companionship Model

Instead of the prayer of petition which has had pride of place in traditional devotion to the saints, the prayer of praise and thanks to God and the prayer of lament characterize a companionship model. It is not that explicit petition is never made, but such asking assumes a different character when set within a relationship of mutuality rather than a structure of elitism. Prayer for help also diminishes in importance in the context of the larger impulses of imbibing encouragement from the saints' witness and praying in profound gratitude for their lives and in lament over their destruction. While thanking God for the witness of the saints is part of the liturgical heritage, complaint to God over the historical treatment suffered by many of them has not customarily been associated with this symbol. Both forms flow today in practices of hopeful remembrance.

Thanks

With the belief that every good gift comes from the generous hand of the One who creates and saves the world, hearty thanks to the Giver characterizes Jewish and Christian prayer from the beginning. People bless God for the wonders of creation, the gift of a plentiful harvest, safe delivery in childbirth, relationships healed, peace established, justice attained, health recovered, and for the transforming gifts of divine mercy and redeeming grace. Indeed, the whole orientation of liturgical prayer is in this direction. The subversive memory of the cloud of witnesses leads in this same direction of gratitude and praise when their historical reality is appreciated in light of its deepest truth, their ever so individual response to amazing grace. As an example of the prayer of thanks, the *Oxford Book of Prayer* cites the following:

> We thank thee, O God, for the saints of all ages; for those who in times of darkness kept the lamp of faith burning; for the great souls who saw visions of larger truth and dared to declare it; for the multitude of quiet

and gracious souls whose presence has purified and
sanctified the world; and for those known and loved by
us, who have passed from this earthly fellowship into the
fuller light of life with thee.[1]

Profound gratitude to God for these women
and men who are our honor recognizes that what
makes them remarkable, both those known and those
unknown, stems from the power of the Spirit who has
had a greening effect on their lives, to use Hildegard of
Bingen's metaphor, keeping them from being dried out
sticks and filling them with the juice of life. The prayer
also implies that the community today is similarly
gifted. People still keep faith burning in the darkness,
speak truth to power, and live gracefully in this world;
loved ones still die and go forth with our hope clinging
to them. Thanking God for these lives is a theocentric
way of expressing the phenomenon of connectedness in
the Spirit.

Lament

Reclaiming the communion of saints as all saints
brings yet another aspect to the fore: the senseless,
terrified, anonymous, tragic deaths of too many whose
destruction does not even have the saving grace of

witnessing to a cause which they held dear. Human death by famine, torture, war, genocide, and one-on-one violence and the death of living creatures and earth's life systems by human cruelty and greed disrupt the harmony of one generation's witness to the next. Such victimization introduces unmitigated evil into the picture. It cries to heaven for justice, for relief, at least for explanation, which is never forthcoming. The ancient prayer of lament, flung in outrage and grief to God, arises from remembrance of these things. Well attested by the psalms, Hagar's complaint, Jeremiah's lamentations, the tears of the companions of the daughter of Jephthah, Job's challenge to heaven, and Jesus's godforsaken cry from the cross, lament is curiously lacking from Christian practices of prayer, especially liturgical prayer. But the powerful memory of those who died senseless deaths deprived of dignity demands that the praise of God be suffused with their tragedy. In the process, as we gather them into our common memory and hope, they become something more than faceless, forgotten individuals but enter into a living history.

When the tragically dead are remembered in the context of Christian faith, the cross of Jesus introduces a hope that transforms these raw depths of unreason and suffering into doxology, only now the praise is forever imbued with the knowledge of unimaginable pain and the darkness of hope against hope. That which is remembered in grief can be redeemed, made whole, through the promise of the Spirit's new creation. And so we affirm a future for all the nameless dead in the hands of the living God.

The challenge of the prayer of lament is not simply to commend the victims of murderous death to heavenly blessedness, however, but to give their memory a place in the making of a just society and a compassionate world here and now. The disorientation of lament has a critical edge. By the way the church remembers, it allows the past of all the dead to function as raw material for a future of promise. It commits itself to seeing, as theologian David Power writes, "that out of their lives on earth, out of the apparent absurdity of their death, a future comes that belongs to the realization of covenant justice here on earth."[2] The prayer of lament—unreserved protest, sadness, impassioned questioning, strong cry against suffering, and tenderness for the defeated—becomes a social force confronting unjust ideologies and structures. It calls us out of passivity into active engagement against all premature death caused by human beings. Along with the prayer of praise, it shifts our responsibility to praxis.

NOTES

1. Anonymous, in *The Oxford Book of Prayer*, ed. George Appleton (Oxford: Oxford University Press, 1985), 168.
2. David Power, "Calling Up the Dead," in "The Spectre of Mass Death," special issue, *Concilium: International Journal of Theology*, no. 3 (1993): 114.

THE JESUS PRAYER
A WAY TO INNER STILLNESS

Joseph Wong, OSB, CAM

TODAY, ONE OF THE MAJOR CHALLENGES of trying to be a contemplative while living in a modern city is learning how to cultivate inner silence, or inner stillness, in the midst of the clamor and the hectic activities of a busy life. Yet I have known from childhood that the kind of recollectedness which can lead to inner stillness can in fact be maintained in an urban setting. I grew up in Hong Kong, and I used to hear my grandmother, who was a devout Buddhist, reciting the Buddha's name throughout the day. Turning her prayer beads in her hand, she would chant "Nan-Mu E-Mi-To-Fo" (which means "Homage to the Buddha Amitabha"). When I greeted her, she would interrupt her recitation, exchange a few words with me, and then continue chanting "Nan-Mu E-Mi-To-Fo." Later I attended a Catholic school and became a Catholic. When I first learned about the Jesus Prayer, I was greatly struck by the similarities between this prayer and my grandmother's recitation of the Buddha's name. Here, I shall present the Jesus Prayer as a way that can lead us to inner stillness and unceasing prayer, whether we are living in a city or in the countryside.

The Jesus Prayer—also known as the Prayer of the Heart—had its origin in the tradition of the desert monks in fourth-century Egypt. Later, having passed through Mount Sinai, the Jesus Prayer was introduced to Greece, where it flourished on Mount Athos during the Middle Ages. From there it spread to Eastern Europe and became an important element of Eastern Orthodox spirituality. In the middle of the last century it entered the Western Church and is now widely known and practiced in the West as well.

Many Christians have learned about the Jesus Prayer through the nineteenth-century Russian classic *Way of a Pilgrim*, which has been translated into some forty languages. Its anonymous author teaches the Jesus Prayer by way of telling stories about himself. One day when he was in church, so the narrative begins, he heard the Scripture reading of St. Paul's injunction to the Christians to "pray without ceasing" (1 Thess. 5:17). Inspired by the Holy Spirit, the pilgrim felt that Paul's words were addressed to him personally. He was determined to put the command into practice, but first he needed to learn how to cultivate unceasing prayer. He frequented a number of churches and listened to famous preachers for some time, but he was greatly disappointed because no one presented any practical instruction in how to pray unceasingly. Finally, by the grace of God, he met an elderly monk in a small village who taught him the Jesus Prayer as a concrete way of praying continuously. The monk also gave him a copy of the Philokalia, which contained the teachings on the Jesus Prayer given by ancient spiritual masters. Thus, under the guidance of this spiritual father, the pilgrim read the Philokalia with great interest and thereafter recited the Jesus Prayer continuously as he pursued his path as a pilgrim. Then, after a period of time, due to his earnestness, and with the special assistance of the Holy Spirit, the pilgrim was able to obtain the gift of unceasing prayer.

The standard formula of the Jesus Prayer is: "Lord Jesus Christ, Son of God, have mercy on me." In practice, various forms are used. For example, the designation "a sinner" may be added to the ending: "Have mercy on me, a sinner." Some omit the title, "Son of God," and say: "Lord Jesus Christ, have mercy on me." Or the prayer can be simply shortened to the following invocation: "Lord Jesus, have mercy."

How to Pray the Jesus Prayer

The Jesus Prayer is normally practiced in two different ways: structured and spontaneous. The structured way of reciting the Jesus Prayer is to set aside a period of time every day, such as twenty or thirty minutes. The spontaneous way of reciting the Jesus Prayer is to freely repeat the prayer throughout the day. As the two ways complement each other, spiritual masters normally recommend adopting both ways, especially for beginners. After spending some set time every day in saying the Jesus Prayer, the prayer will gradually accompany us in our daily living. That is, the holy name of Jesus will spontaneously appear on our lips and in our hearts at different times and on different occasions throughout the day.

The Jesus Prayer is a way, proven over the centuries, to achieve *hesychia,* a Greek word that means "watchfulness" or "inner stillness" and unceasing prayer. As a prayer of the heart, the Jesus Prayer is a concrete expression of the Holy Spirit praying continuously in the hearts of Christians, "with sighs too deep for words" (Rom. 8:26).

INTERCESSORY PRAYER

A PRACTICE OF PRAYING FOR OTHERS

Ann Ulanov and Barry Ulanov

ALL PRAYER IS SOCIAL. We discover this when we pray for others. Whom do we pray for? What is this zone of mutuality we share with others, on which our being depends? Who intercedes for whom? The whole society of persons who make up our world comes quickly to mind, their hurts and hopes, their causes and failures. We speak of them to God; we lift them up to God; we entrust them to God, and often enough they do the same for us.

We pray for those we love because we must. We know that our love is not powerful enough to protect them from all harm, from all illness, from all evil, from death. Our love is not omnipotent. Our care for them, our insistence that they must have a good life, a full life, a life lived from the center of themselves, forces us to intercede with God on their behalf. By ourselves we cannot guarantee them much. We cannot even prevent our own faults from hurting them. We cannot restrain our own strong hopes and pressures so that they can find and live their own idea of the good life instead of the one we have ordained for them. When we recognize these limiting effects of our love, it is that very love for our children, our dear friends, our husband or wife that impels us beyond ourselves to confide their souls into God's keeping. Praying for them changes our love from a closed to an open hand, from a hand that tightly holds them under rein to one that holds them loosely. Praying for them makes us supple and flexible in our love for them.

We learn to pray for those we dislike and avoid as well, for those we hate and fear, for our enemies. Such prayer shifts our attention from all the things others have done to us or neglected to do that so wounded or enraged us, to focus on what it is in ourselves that permits others to acquire such power over us, the power to put us, in effect, in the hell of anger, or dismay, or insecurity, or fear. Prayer for them directs us to the antecedent attitudes or conditions of personality in ourselves that deliver us over into others' power.

Praying for our enemies changes our attitudes toward them. Enemies make us bring light into painful hidden corners of ourselves that we would prefer to leave dark. By trying to put ourselves in another person's shoes, we may discover what we do that so irritates others and makes them dislike us. We hear new voices in our prayer that usually we tune out. We see ourselves from a different angle, one we could not find either by ourselves or with the help of friends. Only enemies can help us here. In this way they are priceless.

Intercession leads us to pray also for the dead. We pray for a father, a mother, a grandmother, or an aunt who loved us and helped us be by really seeing us as we were and rejoicing in our own special personhood, not because it was so superior or gifted, not because it caused such worry or fear, but simply because it was. They were glad in us, glad for what we were, and communicated to us their grateful joy of acceptance at the most basic level. This kind of acceptance makes life exciting because when we are met and greeted in this way we feel real, alive, and delighted to be our very own self. Praying for the souls of such persons, in death as in life, releases into life a fullness of gratitude for their existence. We pray for their joy, their salvation, their immediacy to divine presence, their being-at-the-core in whatever form of resurrected life exists for them.

In praying for those already dead, we open to our own dying, to the undoing of our life in its present forms. We give over control and we unravel the cares of this life, quieting down to admit the fears of letting go into the unknown. Praying for the dead makes a bridge in us to the death that awaits us and makes room for our uncertainties and fears. And contemplating death curiously enough calls us into life more fully, to live it right up to the end because we free our energies from the fear of death to the devotion to life.

We further pray for those we meet who are suffering or will suffer, that we may be attentive, neither interfering with hasty solutions that really only cut off other persons' displaying to us how deeply they suffer, nor quitting the scene because we cannot stand their pain. Such prayers open unlived parts of ourselves, interceding for easier access for them to our consciousness and thus to our development. We open the windows wide to see what will come in from the outside and what will come out from the inside.

Prayer enters the non-space, non-time zone, that part of our life that knows no boundaries and partakes of the timelessness of God's eternity. There, each moment exists in a permanent "now," standing out from other moments as all there is. Thus we can pray across the limitations of time and space. Intercessory prayer pulls us into the tow of God's connectedness to everything.

We are pulled into a current that shows us nothing is separated from anything else, no one from everyone else. Not only do we discover the hungry parts of ourselves that we need to feed when we pray for the hungry persons of the world, but we discover the neglected parts of the world through praying into being the neglected parts of ourselves.

As we pray for those who concretely come across our path, into our road—those within our immediate world and those without, those of the past and those of the future—the whole question of whether our prayers change other people rearranges itself. When we try to pray for others, we are clear we are changed ourselves. We open up, we soften, we put into perspective hurts they have dealt us. We enter their lives now from their point of view instead of exclusively from our own, and as a result we are introduced increasingly to God's point of view, a remarkable vantage point from which to see their lives and our own. The question of causality (did our prayer do this for them?) dissolves in this increasing current of God's interconnectedness with all of us and our intensified awareness of it in all the parts of our lives.

We live the meaning of the mystical body of Christ in this interconnectedness of intercession, where our pleas

for others become pleas for ourselves and their pleas
for themselves become pleas for us. We know by direct
experience that we are, as St. Paul says, members one of
another. One further confirmation of this extraordinary
fact comes to us if in our development of intercessory
prayer, we move into the prayer of free association. In
it, we bring together whatever names and concerns come
to our minds—or to our hearts or souls—as soon as we
have selected our first name, our first person, for whom
to pray. Others follow in remarkably fast order in a rich,
gladdening discourse with the Spirit, each name suggesting another, and another, and another, directly connected
or loosely connected or not connected at all except in
our prayer. We do not have to hunt for people, or worry
about what may be bothering them, or work at it with
any degree of intensity. They will come to us, the people
who should be filling our prayers, the needs they have
or have had or are likely to have. Some of them may
have been absent from our thoughts for years or even
decades. Many of them we may have forgotten we ever
knew. We will be surprised and occasionally disturbed,
but we will almost always feel filled up, enlarged, and
supported in ourselves by the experience. Our past and
present and future come together here in this procession
of the Spirit engendered by our prayers.

CENTERING PRAYER

A TREASURE FOR THE SOUL

Joseph G. Sandman

WHO COULD HAVE PREDICTED twenty-five years ago, when three Trappist monks from a monastery in Massachusetts introduced contemplative prayer to a group of "non-contemplatives," that its popularity would grow so dramatically? Today, thousands of believers from a variety of Christian denominations in every state and in dozens of countries practice contemplative prayer daily. In addition, an international network of dedicated volunteers teaches it around the world.

These monks dreamed of taking the church's rich, centuries-old tradition of contemplative prayer and distilling it into a simple, easily learned prayer that ordinary people could practice. They believed that the daily practice of this prayer could lead to a more intimate union with God and a more powerful experience of God's presence in our lives. This active presence heals, transforms, and offers freedom and peace. Today, many Christians throughout the world are deeply committed to the daily practice called "centering prayer," which they experience as a cornerstone of their lives.

What Is Centering Prayer?

Centering prayer is a remarkably simple method that opens one to God's gift of contemplative prayer. Its practice expands one's receptivity to the presence and activity of God in one's life. It is a distillation of the practice of monastic spirituality into two relatively short periods of prayer each day.

The experience of thousands of practitioners has convinced most centering prayer teachers that two periods a day of twenty to thirty minutes each are necessary to enable the believer to benefit fully from the practice. At the start of a session, the practitioner has the intention to rest deeply in God in silence and to let go of the thoughts, emotions, memories, images, or sensations that will inevitably come into awareness during prayer. The fundamental dynamic of centering prayer is not to stop thinking or to combat thoughts as they arise, but rather to let them go gently so they can pass through one's awareness. Thus the believer can return with his or her whole being to an awareness of God.

The Fruits of Centering Prayer

A growing body of literature describes the benefits of practicing centering prayer. Since the principal arena for living a spiritual life is not prayer but rather everyday life, the benefits of centering prayer reveal themselves not during periods of prayer, but over time in the way we live our lives.

The essence of centering prayer is consent to the presence and activity of God in one's life. In response to our intention to become more deeply united with the divine presence, God acts within us to transform us, making us more like Christ. One's intimacy with God deepens and one's awareness of that intimacy expands.

Those who regularly practice centering prayer have identified its many benefits. These include: greater access to God's own wisdom and energy; a significant increase in creativity; a decrease in compulsive behavior; a reduction of painful emotions and negative thoughts and greater freedom to respond positively to them when they do arise; a greater ability to accept difficult situations with peace and joy; an expanded capacity to accept others on their own terms without judging them or desiring them to change; an ability to love others more selflessly; and a greater awareness of the presence of God in every person and situation we encounter.

Leaders of Contemplative Outreach (www.centering prayer.com), an organization dedicated to the practice of centering prayer, predict that this prayer form will continue to grow because it is a simple, effective, and powerful way to access a deeper relationship with God and because it addresses a hunger within the hearts and souls of individuals who long for peace and a deep experience of God in a fast-paced, impersonal, competitive, and often hostile world.

Four Simple Steps to Practice Centering Prayer

1. Choose a sacred word as the symbol of your intention to consent to God's presence and action within.

2. Sitting comfortably with eyes closed, settle briefly and silently and introduce the sacred word as the symbol of your consent to God's presence and action within.

3. When you become aware of thoughts, return ever so gently to the sacred word.

4. At the end of the prayer period, remain in silence with eyes closed for a couple of minutes.

THE ROSARY
RECALLING THE CHRISTIAN
MYSTERIES OF FAITH

Thomas H. Groome

LIKE MANY CATHOLICS, I grew up in a family that recited the rosary every night. And we knew why we did; as Mom would often assure us, the most effective person to take our prayers to Jesus was his own mother. As a good son, how could he refuse her?

As children, we often came to the nightly rosary with protest—"in a minute, Ma"—but having settled on our knees, it was a lovely, quieting time, one that bonded our family of nine kids at the end of a day of the usual sibling tensions. Years later, when we gathered for our parents' wakes, and then for those of siblings, we prayed the rosary together and it bonded us still. The rosary crusader Father Paddy Peyton was right when he said, "The family that prays together, stays together."

The gentle drone of the Hail Marys helped introduce me to what I later knew as meditation. My mother
would encourage us to "just think about the mysteries." How wise she was. In his lovely apostolic letter
Rosarium Virginis Mariae (RVM), Pope John Paul II
called the rosary "a path of contemplation."

If one of us missed the family recitation, our mother's
good night was always accompanied by "Be sure to say
your rosary." We knew that she kept her own beads under
her pillow for waking moments. And my grandmother
loved to assure us that if you start the rosary and then fall
asleep, "the angels and saints finish it for you."

From my childhood, then, I knew the rosary as both
communal and personal prayer, as a quieting mantra-
like mode of recitation and contemplation. It convinced
me that we can go to Jesus through Mary, and that a
great communion of saints prays with us. It taught me
the responsibility of praying by myself as well as with
others; it taught me that I could pray just about any time
and any place.

The rosary can have all of these catechetical benefits
for postmodern people, in addition to its powerful
efficacy as a mode of prayer. Its widespread popularity
fell off after Vatican II—an unintended outcome of the
Council's efforts to refocus Catholics on Jesus, sacred

Scripture, and the liturgy. But as Pope John Paul II noted in RVM, the rosary, "though clearly Marian in character, at heart is a Christocentric prayer" and "has all the depth of the Gospel message in its entirety."

What garnered attention for RVM was that Pope John Paul added five new mysteries to the rosary. For some 500 years, the full rosary consisted of fifteen decades, each one focused on some mystery from the life of Christ or Mary. Then, the fifteen decades were grouped into three sets of five—called a chaplet, meaning crown—designated as the Joyful, Sorrowful, and Glorious mysteries, and focusing on the incarnation, passion, and glorification of Jesus Christ, respectively. Prior to RVM, there were no mysteries designated for the public life and ministry of Jesus—an enormous gap. I rejoiced when Pope John Paul II announced the addition of five new mysteries focused precisely on the life of Jesus. As Catholics pray these Mysteries of Light—or Luminous mysteries—we are likely to deepen our recognition of, and commitment to, living as disciples of Jesus now.

History of the Rosary

We cannot pinpoint how or when the rosary began as a popular devotion. The old tradition that it was

personally delivered to St. Dominic by the Blessed
Mother herself is now seriously questioned. On the
other hand, the Dominicans certainly helped to stan-
dardize and popularize it throughout the fifteenth and
sixteenth centuries. Pope Pius V, a Dominican, instituted
the feast of Our Lady of the Rosary (now celebrated on
October 7); he credited the efficacy of the rosary with
the defeat of the Turks at the battle of Lepanto in 1571.

Around the year 1000, ordinary people began to
recite 150 Our Fathers, divided into three sets of 50 and
counted on strings of beads called paternosters. This
became known as "the poor man's Psalter" because they
were copying the monks and nuns who recited the 150
psalms each day. As Marian devotion increased in the
twelfth century, the Carthusians and Cistercians helped
develop and popularize a rosary of Hail Marys.

Historically, the rosary emerged from the instinct
of ordinary Christians that they, too, were called to the
practice of regular prayer and to sanctify their time and
work throughout the day. They knew the monks and
nuns were doing so with their recitation of the Divine
Office of the Church. But the peasant people didn't have
the time to pause for choral reading. Their instinct was
to insist on praying themselves. The rosary arose from
the good sense of ordinary people that Baptism calls all

to holiness of life, and this demands the regular practice of prayer.

How to Pray the Rosary

What is the best way to say the rosary? The tradition is to meditate on the mystery of each decade rather than to focus on the words of each prayer. So, with the first Joyful mystery, the Annunciation, one can think about God's great initiative here, about Mary's openness to doing God's will, and so on. Or, more contemplatively, one can imagine and enter into the setting as the Angel Gabriel appears to Mary, listen in to the exchange between them, and so on. The purpose of all such contemplation is to take the mystery into daily life to encourage Christian discipleship. As Pope John Paul II wisely commented, we have in the rosary "a treasure to be rediscovered."

It is customary to assign each chaplet to a particular day of the week. *Rosarium Virginis Mariae* (RVM) suggests that the Joyful mysteries be prayed on Monday and Saturday, the Luminous on Thursday, the Sorrowful on Tuesday and Friday, and the Glorious on Wednesday and Sunday.

One popular opening prayer is the first verse of Psalm 70, "O God, come to my assistance. O Lord, make haste to help me." A variation of the opening prayer is to say the Apostles' Creed.

This is followed by an Our Father, three Hail Marys, and a Glory Be. Then announce the chaplet and the first mystery, for example, "The five Joyful mysteries, the first mystery, the Annunciation." After announcing each mystery, pause for the proclamation of a related biblical passage, and silence for meditation. Then follow with the Our Father, the decade of Hail Marys, and the Glory Be for each of the five mysteries.

The Joyful Mysteries

1. Annunciation by Gabriel to the Virgin Mary
2. Visitation of Mary to Elizabeth
3. Birth of the Savior of the world
4. Presentation of Jesus in the temple
5. Finding of twelve-year-old Jesus in the temple

The Luminous Mysteries

1. Baptism of Jesus
2. Jesus at the wedding of Cana
3. Jesus proclaims the Kingdom of God
4. Jesus's transfiguration
5. Jesus institutes the Eucharist

The Sorrowful Mysteries

1. Anguish of Jesus in Gethsemane
2. Jesus is scourged
3. Jesus is crowned with thorns
4. Jesus carries his cross
5. Jesus dies on the cross

The Glorious Mysteries

1. Resurrection of Jesus from the dead
2. Jesus ascends into glory
3. The Spirit outpours upon Mary and the disciples at Pentecost
4. Mary is assumed into Heaven
5. Mary shines forth as Queen of the Angels and Saints

There are different ways to conclude. Typical, however, is to end with the Hail Holy Queen or Memorare.

Hail, Holy Queen

Hail, holy Queen, Mother of Mercy! Our life, our sweetness, and our hope! To thee do we cry, poor banished children of Eve, to thee do we send up our sighs, mourning and weeping in this valley of tears. Turn, then, most gracious advocate, thine eyes of mercy toward us. And after this our exile, show unto us the blessed fruit of thy womb, Jesus; O clement, O loving, O sweet virgin Mary, pray for us, O holy Mother of God, that we may be made worthy of the promises of Christ.

Memorare

Remember, O most gracious Virgin Mary, that never was it known that anyone who fled to your protection, implored your help, or sought your intercession was left unaided. Inspired with this confidence, I fly to you, O virgin of virgins, my Mother. To you I come, before you I kneel, sinful and sorrowful. O Mother of the Word Incarnate, despise not my petitions; but in your mercy, hear and answer me. Amen.

LITURGY OF THE HOURS

GIVING RHYTHM TO OUR DAYS

Elizabeth Collier

HAVING SPENT THE PAST FIFTEEN YEARS at various Jesuit institutions, I have probably logged more hours on retreats, in spiritual direction, in prayer groups, discussing or teaching theological topics, and doing or organizing service work than your average thirtysomething. But despite all of the above, I am embarrassed to say that for the past few years I have not spent much time praying, and when I have it has not been as fruitful as I would like. This is due, in large part, to the pace of my life. As with many people I know, I am overcommitted, juggle too much responsibility, and collapse at night very much aware of all I was not able to accomplish during the day.

To fill the void of my poor prayer life, I have often browsed through the many meditation books and resources for "busy people," but nothing I have tried has satisfied more than a feeling of fulfilling an obligation. My search was more for something with the depth and beauty that so many other aspects of our faith can offer. But how to find a middle ground among my spiritual desires, the scriptural call to "pray ceaselessly," and the constraints on my time and energy?

Last spring, the U.S. Cistercian novice directors asked my husband and me to meet with them in Snowmass, Colorado, to help them better understand Generation X. Having no experience with cloistered religious, I arrived at the meeting somewhat skeptical, even suspicious, of their vocation. The Jesuit charism surrounding social justice and phrases like "contemplatives in action" were what encapsulated my ideals of Christian service. I did not understand how a cloistered life was a "ministry" to the church or the world, or how monastic men and women were "bringing about the kingdom of God." But after several days of meetings, meals, and late-night conversations, I came to admire the Cistercian life and saw many more connections between our two vocations than I would have imagined. These were healthy, interesting, intelligent, and deeply spiritual people, whose time living in a community of work and prayer had given them insights into their own talents as well as the challenges they faced within their communities.

Cistercian time is punctuated by praying the Liturgy of the Hours and by practicing mindfulness during the day's work. And although I am not called to their particular vocation, I longed for a way of marking my own days with similar rhythms of prayer.

After returning to Chicago, I committed myself to more regular prayer. In my home library, I found a two-volume set of books that I had bought several years before but had never used: a layperson's guide to the Liturgy of the Hours. I decided to take up the texts on my own terms, adapting them to my vocation and lifestyle without learning the rubrics or even much of the history. I did not want to get caught up in "shoulds," but wanted to explore how God might be able to break into my contemporary life through this ages-old tradition. Morning and evening prayers include several psalms, a brief reading from a saint, theologian, or spiritual writer, a responsorial psalm, the canticle of Zechariah or of Mary, prayer petitions, and a short prayer to begin or end the day.

After spending time with these prayers and, later, learning more about the history of the Liturgy of the Hours, I found many aspects of the office particularly suited to much of what I had been seeking. With its roots in ancient Jewish rituals, its later adaptation by the early Christian community, and its continued use daily throughout Christian history, I felt a profound historical connection with the countless generations who have punctuated their days in similar ways.

Especially valuable for me is the prayer experience offered by the particular version I use. It combines ancient psalms and canticles, readings from the church fathers, medieval saints, and modern women, and intercessions that relate to the challenges of contemporary socioeconomic structures and environmental concerns.

The development of the devotion over time also exemplified the adaptability and flexibility for which I had been searching. From as early as the fourth and fifth centuries, attempts by the laity to integrate regular prayer times with their urban lives resulted in the flowering of different traditions for praying the Liturgy of the Hours. A monastic lifestyle allowed for a more frequent and time-intensive focus on the psalms and prayer periods throughout the day and night. In turn, an urban cathedral tradition developed for the laity, which called people to pray as a community in the morning and the evening and included shorter meditations and fewer psalms. This tradition accommodated the workaday life of the average person. But from the twelfth century on, outside of monasteries, the practice became primarily a private, clerical devotion. The laity focused on shorter prayers and devotions like the rosary, which could be done either privately or within the church community. Today, priests and deacons are still required to pray the Liturgy of the Hours daily, and the Second Vatican Council called for the devotion to be incorporated more into parish life.

In addition to the historical tradition of the devotion, it moves me deeply to think that people throughout the world, from all walks of life, are praying with similar texts each day. This provides an almost tangible connectedness that inspires me in the solitude of my home office. When I am able to pray in the morning, it brings a mindfulness to the gift of the day, which often stays with me after I walk out the door. The text itself provides not only the comforting repetition found in the Mass, but also enough variety that I have less of a tendency to "go through the motions," as I do with other forms of prayer. By following the liturgical year, I feel connected to the seasons of the church year in a way that I enjoyed when daily Mass was still an option for my schedule. And the readings for feast days allow me an opportunity to gain insight into the lives of inspiring men and women. Overall, the various types of prayers and readings touch upon the struggles and celebrations that occur in the lives of us all.

Admittedly, I do not pray the Liturgy of the Hours as diligently as I might, nor do I replicate the total commitment of the monastic communities. But the connectedness I feel to a larger praying community helps with this. If I can pray only once a day or miss prayer altogether, I know that thousands of others are carrying on this living tradition for the good of all creation. If I begin praying the office and discover an image or phrase that calls my attention, my Ignatian education kicks in and I realize that God is drawing me toward a more specific word to focus on that day. And on days when I actually pray the morning, afternoon, and evening hours, I know that I have taken up the call to prayer for those who did not have time or were for other reasons unable to pray.

It is ironic that a trip intended to offer a cloistered community insight into a generation that grew up in the midst of instant entertainment and constant activity would result in my incorporating an ancient contemplative practice into my Ignatian-influenced, action-oriented Christian life. It seems a special testament to a Spirit who brings forward elements of our tradition that have been life-giving for previous generations in ways that are fruitful and adaptable in the midst of contemporary challenges.

Getting Started—Morning and Evening Prayer

• Begin by praying several psalms.

• Followed by a brief reading from a saint, theologian, or spiritual writer.

• Pray one more psalm. This is called a responsorial psalm, such as the canticle of Zechariah or of Mary.

• Then, add your own prayer petitions, and a short prayer to begin or end the day.

PRAYING WITH IMAGES
ON WHAT MEETS THE EYE

Colleen M. Griffith

A PICTURE IS WORTH A THOUSAND WORDS." So the saying goes, and historical Christians were quick to grasp this. They recognized the formative power of visual images, particularly the way that images gathered the energy and affect of worshippers, stimulating their desire to deepen in a Christian way of life.

Twenty-first-century Christians have less experience utilizing visual images as a spiritual resource. It's not that we are image starved. We're barraged by massive doses of media images and we've grown accustomed to this. Press photographs and advertising images surround us on a daily basis, orienting us to events of our world and forming our attitudes and desires at conscious and unconscious levels. But are our spiritual selves formed by these images? What critical and faith perspectives are we bringing to the media images to which we've become habituated? And what visual images are we intentionally choosing to contemplate precisely for their formative influence on our lives of faith?

Image as Spiritual Resource

Visual images are evocative because with directness and brevity, they "speak" volumes in their expressiveness. Images appeal to emotions and exert influence on the viewer. The prayerful contemplation of a religious image can mediate a rich encounter with God. In beholding an image over time, we come into a new sense of perspective and catch sight of fresh points of direction. Visual images give us powerful access to feelings that operate below the surface and can become the stuff of prayer.

Images that carry spiritual meaning do not all fall under the heading "religious art," understood in a traditional sense. Iconic art, representational images, impressionistic works, and nonrepresentational abstract works have all proven formative in orienting persons' spiritual lives. What matters most, it seems, is choosing an image that attracts and invites contemplation.

Praying with Visual Images

How does one utilize visual images in prayer? To begin, choose an image with which to spend time, preferably one with strong expressive power to which you can respond effectively. Second, do your best to avoid any premature fixing of interpretation of your image. Instead, contemplate it with a spirit of openness and expectancy. Third, notice the memories, associations, and longings to which your image gives rise. In doing so, allow the affective dimensions of your image full sway. Pray then out of the full engagement of your senses and the feelings evoked by your image.

We can't expect visual images to clarify points or supply us with decisions; they won't. We can, however, expect that having a regular practice of praying with visual images will form and inform our discipleship, training our religious affections. Latino/a Catholic communities have taken a strong lead in underscoring the material mediation of the sacred in visual terms and demonstrating how in parish and home settings, religious images can play a crucial role. It is time now for all of us to reclaim the historic Christian understanding of the spiritually formative function of images. By developing a repertoire of images with which we can pray, images that nurture our spirits and beckon us to live more authentic lives, we, in a consumerist, media-driven culture, catch sight of an alternative to the uncritical acceptance of all that passes in front of our eyes.

The Power of Icons

Icons are a particular type of visual image with which Christians pray. Visual images bearing the name "icon" are painted in a distinctive style and from an accompanying posture of prayer and reflection. Manuals of iconography from the second millennium offer detailed instructions regarding the writing of icons, precise guidelines pertaining to particular forms, features, and colors of Christ and the saints. Icons are not decorations but holders of sacred history that serve a sacramental function. Through icons, persons in prayer enter sacred time and place moving toward communion with the mystery signified. This is holy practice. In praying with icons, one comes to fresh insight and perception into reality. The world of icons discloses the eternal dimension present in the realm of sense and experience. The icon bespeaks an inner vision where the material and the spiritual meet, where creation and divinity are one. Being thick signifiers with many layers of meaning, icons remind us that we are living in a Spirit-filled world and are formed by God's love in Christ. These powerful examples of sacred imagery affirm the mystery of the Incarnation, reminding us of the grace-filled dimensions of Christ's bodiliness and our own. Iconography remains a longstanding constitutive dimension of the theology, worship, and spirituality of Eastern Orthodox Christians.

Getting Started—Praying with Images

- Select an image or icon. Frequently an image will almost select you.
- Sit or stand before the visual image, allowing it to point you in the direction of the presence of God.
- If your image portrays a saint, invite that saint to be a companion and guide.
- Pray a closing prayer that rises from your heart, or pray the Jesus Prayer or the Lord's Prayer.

EVERYDAY PRAYERS

BY HEART

Compiled by
Thomas H. Groome

"Prayer is the raising of the mind and heart to God."
   (St. Therese of Lisieux)

*"It is right and good to pray so that the coming of the
kingdom of justice and peace may influence the march
of history, but it is just as important to bring the help
of prayer into humble, everyday situations; all forms of
prayer can be the leaven to which the Lord compares
the kingdom."*
   (*Catechism of the Catholic Church*, #2660)

The Lord's Prayer

Our Father, who art in heaven, hallowed be Thy name:
Thy kingdom come; Thy will be done on earth as it is in
heaven. Give us this day our daily bread; and forgive us

our trespasses as we forgive those who trespass against us; and lead us not into temptation, but deliver us from evil. Amen.

The Hail Mary

Hail Mary, full of grace, the Lord is with you; blessed are you among women, and blessed is the fruit of your womb, Jesus. Holy Mary, Mother of God, pray for us sinners now and at the hour of our death. Amen.

Glory Be . . .

Glory be to the Father, and to the Son, and to the Holy Spirit: as it was in the beginning, is now, and will be forever. Amen.

Prayer to the Holy Spirit

Come, Holy Spirit, fill the hearts of your faithful. And kindle in them the fire of your love. Send forth your Spirit and they shall be created. And you will renew the face of the earth. Let us pray, O God, by the light of the Holy Spirit you have taught the hearts of your faithful. In the same spirit, let us relish what is right, and always rejoice in your consolation. We ask this through Christ our Lord. Amen.

Morning Prayer

Loving God, thank you for the gift of this new day. I offer you all my thoughts, words, actions, joys, and sorrows of this day so that your kingdom may come and your will be done on earth as it is in heaven. Amen.

Night Prayer

Lord Jesus Christ, accept the prayers and works of this day. Give us now the rest that will strengthen us to render more faithful service to you, who live and reign, for ever and ever. Amen.

Grace before Meals

Bless us, O Lord, and these your gifts which we are about to receive from your goodness. Through Christ our Lord. Amen.

Act of Contrition

My God, I am sorry for my sins with all my heart. In choosing to do wrong and failing to do good, I have sinned against you whom I should love above all things. I firmly intend, with your help, to do penance, to sin no more, and to avoid whatever leads me to sin. Our Savior Jesus Christ suffered and died for us. In his name, my God, have mercy. Amen.

Hail, Holy Queen

Hail, holy Queen, mother of mercy, Hail, our life, our sweetness, and our hope. To you we cry, the children of Eve; to you we send up our sighs, mourning and weeping in this land of exile. Turn, then, most gracious advocate, your eyes of mercy toward us; Lead us home at least and show us the blessed Fruit of your womb, Jesus: O clement, O loving, O sweet Virgin Mary.

Saint Patrick's Breastplate

Christ, be with me, Christ before me, Christ behind me, Christ within me, Christ beneath me, Christ above me, Christ on my right, Christ on my left, Christ where I lie, Christ where I sit, Christ where I arise. Christ in the heart of everyone who thinks of me, Christ in the mouth of everyone who speaks to me, Christ in the eye of everyone who sees me, Christ in the ear of everyone who hears me. Amen.

Reflection of Saint Teresa of Avila

Christ has no body now, but yours. No hands, no feet on earth, but yours. Yours are the eyes through which Christ looks compassion into the world. Yours are the feet with which Christ walks to do good. Yours are the hands with which Christ blesses the world.

Prayer of Saint Francis

Lord, make me an instrument of your peace: where there is hatred, let me sow love; where there is injury, pardon; where there is doubt, faith; where there is despair, hope; where there is darkness, light; where there is sadness, joy.

O Divine Master, grant that I may not so much seek to be consoled as to console, to be understood as to understand, to be loved as to love.

For it is in giving that we receive, it is in pardoning that we are pardoned, it is in dying that we are born to eternal life. Amen.

Suscipe

Take, Lord, and receive all my liberty, my memory, my understanding, and my entire will, all I have and call my own. You have given all to me. To you, Lord, I return it. Everything is yours; do with it what you will. Give me only your love and your grace. That is enough for me. (St. Ignatius of Loyola)

PART TWO

PRACTICES *of* CARE

LIVING THE SACRAMENTAL PRINCIPLE

FINDING THE EXTRAORDINARY
IN THE ORDINARY

Esther de Waal

A WOMAN KNEELS on the hard earth floor in her small hut in the Outer Hebrides, those harsh and inhospitable islands lying off the west coast of Scotland. She has already washed by splashing her face with three palmfuls of water (for this is in the nineteenth century), and as she did so she invoked the name of the Trinity.

The palmful of the God of Life
The palmful of the Christ of Love
The palmful of the Spirit of Peace

Triune
of grace.

Now, at daybreak, and before the rest of her family is awake, she starts to do what is her daily chore: to stir into life the fire banked down the night before. Nothing could be more mundane, more prosaic, than this essential household obligation, performed day by day and year by year. Yet by her gestures and her words, she transforms it and brings to the action a deeper meaning. As she works, she says aloud in a quiet crooning to herself:

> I will kindle my fire this morning
> In the presence of the holy angels of heaven.

And as the embers burst into flame, that fire becomes symbolic of the flame of love that we should keep burning for the whole family of humankind.

> God, kindle thou in my heart within
> A flame of love to my neighbor,
> To my foe, to my friend, to my kindred all,
> To the brave, to the knave, to the thrall,
> O Son of the loveliest Mary,
> From the lowliest thing that liveth
> To the name that is highest of all.

She has made the mundane the edge of glory. She has allowed the extraordinary to break in on the ordinary. As "lifting" the peats had been the first duty of the day, so smothering, or "smooring," them is the last. This too becomes a symbolic action, one performed with a sense of a world beyond that with which she is dealing, so that as she handles the peats she is touching something that has its significance at a far deeper level. She divides the peats into three sections, one for each member of the Trinity. Then she lays down the first in the name of the God of Life, the second in the name of the God of Peace, and the third in the name of the God of Grace. She next covers the circle of peat with ashes, enough to subdue but not extinguish the fire, in the name of the Three of Light. The slightly raised heap in the center becomes the Hearth of the Three. When this is finished, she closes her eyes, stretches out her hand, and softly intones one of the many smooring prayers.

The Sacred Three

The household

To save

This eve

To shield

This night

To surround

And every night

The hearth

Each single night

The house

Amen.

In doing all this, the woman has been following the Celtic practice handed down from generation to generation (and known to us because it was orally collected at the end of the last century). It was a practice in which ordinary people in their daily lives took the tasks that lay to hand but treated them sacramentally, as pointing to a greater reality that lay beyond them. It is an approach to life that we have been in danger of losing, this sense of allowing the extraordinary to break in on the ordinary. Perhaps it is something that we can rediscover, something which Celtic spirituality can give to us if we would let it renew our vision by teaching our eyes to see again, our ears to hear, our hands to handle. Then, like the disciples on the way to Emmaus who trudged along feeling so disconsolate and let down, we shall discover that Christ was in fact alongside us all the time. The fault lay with us, for we had simply failed to notice.

The Celtic approach to God opens up a world in which nothing is too common to be exalted and nothing is so exalted that it cannot be made common. What a waste it is to be surrounded by heaven, by a sky "made white by angels' wings," and to be unaware of it. Perhaps the first step is that we really should want to unearth God in our midst. For letting heaven break through will not happen automatically. It lies to hand, but it needs a determination on our part to find it. Yet, if we can rediscover this vision, then we too may be able to transform what lies to hand, let the mundane become the edge of glory, and find the extraordinary in the ordinary.

PRACTICING HOSPITALITY

EXTENDING WELCOME
TO THOSE IN NEED

Ana María Pineda, RSM

F OR MANY DECADES, the Mission District of San Francisco has been a home and a welcome *posada* (shelter) for a diverse population of Hispanics and Latinos. Over the years, it has taken on the aged familiarity of the neighborhoods its inhabitants left behind in their Latin American countries of origin. Its streets bustle with activity as people attend to the daily needs of family and work and as children come and go to school. Throughout the day, the bells of St. Peter's announce the presence of the church. The Mission District teems with life, as the culture and customs of the Latino world fill its days with vitality.

On this December evening, children of every age process down Twenty-Fourth Street, some with lighted candles in hand and others carrying on their shoulders statues of Mary and Joseph. Each Advent, the young and the old reenact the story of Joseph seeking lodging for his young wife, Mary, who is weary from travel and heavy with child. For nine nights in a row, children and adults assume the identity of the weary couple or of the innkeepers, processing around the inside of the church or throughout the neighborhood, moving from one designated site to the next. This is the beloved ritual of *Las Posadas*.

At each station, an ancient exchange is repeated. Those playing the role of Joseph approach the inn, knock on the door, and say in a loud voice, *En nombre del cielo, buenos moradores, dad a unos viajeros posada esta noche.* (In the name of heaven, we ask those who dwell here, give to some travelers lodging tonight.) From inside, a chorus of voices responds, *Aquí no es mesón: sigan adelante. Yo no puedo abrir: no sea algún tunante* (This is not an inn; move on—I cannot open because you might be a scoundrel). As Joseph moves from one inn to the next, the innkeepers grow angry and even threaten violence, while the night grows colder and the young couple's weariness turns to exhaustion. *Venimos rendidos desde Nazareth, yo soy carpintero de nombre José* (We are tired traveling from Nazareth; I am a carpenter named Joseph), the anxious husband implores. Finally, he even reveals his wife's true identity, begging for *posada* for just one night for *la Reina del Cielo*, the Queen of Heaven—to no avail.

For eight days, the scene is reenacted. Finally, on the ninth day, the eve of Christmas, Joseph's request moves the heart of an innkeeper, who offers the young couple all that he has left—a stable. Yet the stable is enhanced by the love with which the innkeeper offers it, and this humble place becomes the birthplace of Jesus. In an outpouring of joy and festivity, those gathered on the final night celebrate the generosity of the innkeeper and the *posada* given to Mary and Joseph in song and dance, food and drink. Candy and treats from a piñata shower the children, and the community recalls anew how the stranger at one's door can be God in disguise.

Every December, Hispanic communities relive in their flesh the Gospel truth that "the Word became flesh and lived among us" (John 1:14). "He was in the world, and the world came into being through him; yet the world did not know him. He came to what was his own, and his own people did not accept him" (John 1:10–11). In *Las Posadas*, they ritually participate in being rejected and being welcomed, in slamming the door on the needy and opening it wide. They are in this way renewed in the Christian practice of hospitality, the practice of providing a space where the stranger is taken in and known as one who bears gifts.

Strangers in Our Midst

Although *Las Posadas* is a beautiful, engaging ritual, the reality it addresses is a painful one: the reality of human need and exclusion. When the ritual takes place in the Mission District of San Francisco, many of the participants—once refugees themselves—remember their own experience as strangers. Through the ritual, the community affirms the goodness of taking people in, and those who once needed *posada* are reminded to offer it to others.

This is a lesson that is needed in other communities as well. The need for shelter, for *posada*, is a fundamental human need. None of us ever knows for sure when we might be uprooted and cast on the mercy of others. Throughout human history, there have been times when people were dislocated, becoming vulnerable as they journeyed far from home. Sometimes there have been people to take them in, and sometimes not.

Just as the human need for hospitality is a constant, so, it seems, is the human fear of the stranger. Unfortunately, the fear of "the strange one" has a long history in human societies. The stranger seems to portend danger— sometimes of physical harm, but also because the stranger represents the unknown, a challenge to the familiar constructs of our personal world. And so we human beings try to keep strangers at a distance; we avoid risky encounters or we try to neutralize the stranger's power in order to protect our own. Some societies try to appease strangers with gifts; others exclude or even destroy them.

These fundamental human needs and fears confront contemporary men and women intensely. As the world shrinks and mobility increases, we encounter strangers frequently. But this has only heightened our fears. Those who enjoy comfort and shelter edge their way around homeless strangers. Those whose health is presently strong turn away from the gaunt, blemished faces of those living with AIDS. The prosperous never enter the poverty-stricken neighborhoods that abound with gang violence, drug abuse, unemployment, and welfare dependency. "Strangers" do not belong in the world in which the "comfortable" move with relative ease. And so there is no room for those who do not conform to mainstream standards or speak the mainstream language. Access to borders and to basic resources—shelter, employment, education, and health care—is cut off, as the powerful respond to genuine human need with an inhospitality fueled by fear.

Ironically, it is not just hospitality to the "stranger" that is in peril in our society. We are short not only of tables that welcome strangers but even of tables that welcome friends. In a society that prizes youthfulness, the elderly are often isolated from the affection and care of their own families. In many busy families, children find no after-school welcome home, and spouses find little time to host one another over supper. And when we become estranged—separated by grievances large or small, or simply crowded out of one another's lives—we all too often become "strangers" even to those we once loved. Can we move beyond strangeness and estrangement to learn the skills of welcoming one another and to claim the joy of homecoming?

In the traditions shaped by the Bible, offering hospitality is a moral imperative. The expectation that God's people are people who will welcome strangers and treat them justly runs throughout the Bible. This expectation is not based on any special immunity to the dangers unknown people might present—far from it. Rather, it emerges from knowing the hospitality God has shown to us.

Hospitality Enfleshed:
The Christian Works of Mercy

Corporal Works of Mercy

1. Feed the hungry

2. Give drink to the thirsty

3. Clothe the naked

4. Welcome the stranger

5. Visit the sick and imprisoned

6. Bury the dead

Spiritual Works of Mercy

1. Counsel the doubtful

2. Instruct the ignorant

3. Admonish the sinner

4. Comfort the sorrowful

5. Bear wrongs patiently

6. Pray for the living and the dead

PRACTICING FORGIVENESS

MOVING TOWARD RECONCILIATION

Marjorie J. Thompson

WE SOMETIMES HAVE TROUBLE understanding the precise nature of forgiveness. I would like to begin by suggesting that forgiveness is not certain things with which we often confuse it. Forgiving does not mean denying our hurt. What on the surface appears to be a forgiving attitude may merely reveal that we have succeeded in suppressing our pain. If we bury our hurt or pretend it isn't real, we experience no sense of being wronged that would require our forgiveness. Forgiveness is a possibility only when we acknowledge the negative impact of a person's actions or attitudes on our lives. This holds true whether or not harm was intended by the offender. Until we are honest about our actual feelings, forgiveness has no meaning.

It is important to underscore that forgiveness bears no resemblance to resigned martyrdom. A person with a weak sense of self may too easily take on blame for the actions of others. A person who finds a unique sense of identity by appearing pitiable can learn to play the martyr with great effectiveness. In either case, resignation to the role of victim will prevent any genuine process of forgiveness. If we feel we deserve to be blamed, degraded, or abused, again we will have disguised the offense that needs forgiveness, not by denial but by taking inappropriate responsibility for the offense. One spiritual writer has astutely pointed out that forgiveness does not mean "putting the other one on probation." We may think we have forgiven someone only to catch ourselves waiting impatiently for evidence that the person's behavior merits our clemency. If the offender doesn't measure up to our expectations, the "gift" of mercy is withdrawn: "To grant forgiveness at a moment of softening of the heart, in an emotional crisis, is comparatively easy; not to take it back is something that hardly anyone knows how to do."[1] To forgive is not to excuse an unjust behavior. There are evil and destructive behaviors that are inherently inexcusable: fraud, theft, emotional abuse, physical violence, economic exploitation, or any denial of human rights.

Who could possibly claim that these are excusable? To excuse such behaviors—at least in the sense of winking and pretending not to notice, or of saying "Oh, that's all right," or even "I'll overlook it this time, just don't do it again"—is to tolerate and condone them. Evil actions are manifestly not "all right." They are sins.

Finally, to forgive is not necessarily to forget. Perhaps for small indignities that prick our pride we can simply excuse and forget. But for major assaults that leave us gasping with psychic pain, reeling with the sting of rejection, bowing under the weight of oppressive constraint, or aching with personal loss and grief, we will find ourselves unable either to excuse or to forget. Moreover, there are situations in which it is not desirable to forget. It would be but another expression of arrogance for those of us with European roots to ask Native or African Americans, under the guise of forgiveness, to forget the way they and their ancestors have been treated by the cultural majority in this country. I understand why our Jewish friends insist that we never forget the horrors of the Holocaust. There are brutalities against body, mind, and spirit that must not be forgotten if we are to avoid replaying them. Blows intentionally rendered to crush the vulnerable cannot, humanly speaking, be forgotten. They can, nonetheless, be forgiven.

If we now have greater clarity concerning what forgiveness is not, what then is it? Let me characterize it this way: To forgive is to make a conscious choice to release the person who has wounded us from the sentence of our judgment, however justified that judgment may be. It represents a choice to leave behind our resentment and desire for retribution, however fair such punishment might seem. It is in this sense that one may speak of "forgetting"; not that the actual wound is ever completely forgotten, but that its power to hold us trapped in continual replay of the event, with all the resentment each remembrance makes fresh, is broken.

Moreover, without in any way mitigating the seriousness of the offense, forgiveness involves excusing persons from the punitive consequences they deserve to suffer for their behavior. The behavior remains condemned, but the offender is released from its effects as far as the forgiver is concerned. For the one who releases, such forgiveness is costly both emotionally and spiritually. I believe this reflects in a finite way both the manner in which God forgives us and the costliness of that infinite gift.

Forgiveness constitutes a decision to call forth and rebuild that love which is the only authentic ground of any human relationship. Such love forms the sole secure ground of our relationship with God as well. Indeed, it is only because God continually calls forth and rebuilds this love with us that we are capable of doing so with one another. Thus, to forgive is to participate in the mystery of God's love. Perhaps this is why the old adage rings true: "To err is human; to forgive, divine." Genuine forgiveness draws us right into the heart of divine life.

NOTE

1. Anthony Bloom, *Living Prayer* (Springfield, IL: Templegate Publishers, 1966), 31.

FAMILY LIFE AS SPIRITUAL PRACTICE

DISCIPLINES OF THE DOMESTIC CHURCH

Wendy M. Wright

"It is an error . . . to wish to banish the devout life from the regiment of soldiers, the mechanic's shop, the court of princes, or the home of married persons. True devotion . . . not only does no injury to one's vocation or occupation, but on the contrary adorns and beautifies it." (St. Francis de Sales)

FOR MOST OF US, family life is a busy, bustling life filled with things to do and people to whom to attend. After the birth of our first daughter, I attended a new mother's support group sponsored by the local hospital. Women whose infants had been born at the hospital between six and twelve weeks previous were invited to join. We met on Wednesday mornings at the home of a facilitator to share our experiences. What I remember most about the meetings (besides the carpet full of wiggling, squealing infants) was the common exasperation felt at being so busy. One wide-eyed young matron with twin daughters laughed as she described the highlight of a typical day: finding the time to get outside to the mailbox and bring in the mail. Even a daily shower was an accomplishment. Forget trying to blow-dry hair. Of course, what seems at first to be the all-consuming activity of infant care soon gives away to the ever-vigilant watchfulness of the toddler parent; the bedtime reading sessions of preschool days; the initiation into what will be decades of carpooling; school sports coaching; overseeing homework; keeping doctor, dentist, and orthodontist appointments; and attending parent-teacher conferences. Then there are the high school booster clubs, after-prom committees, math contests, dance recitals, piano lessons, summer soccer leagues, birthday parties, swimming lessons, the never-ending cooking, cleaning, and grocery shopping (for me an almost daily necessity with a teenaged male). Top this off with headaches about insurance premiums, mortgage rates, tuition payments, money for new shoes— the list is endless—and it all adds up to a busy, busy life.

Yet in the midst of the busyness is a strange, wonderful stillness and a silence so full it dwarfs the chatter with which we fill our days. We sense that stillness as snapshot moments: we peer into the nursery of a sleeping infant, or attend the kindergarten class Christmas rendition of "The Friendly Beasts," or watch our high school senior parade across the stage and receive her diploma. In fact, it has been my experience that the very destabilizing of the self-preoccupied "me," the three-hundred-and-sixty-degree rotation in orientation that marriage and parenting bring with them, is in itself an initiation into a realm of being and loving that inches us, if we consciously allow it, into the deep ground of Being and Love that sustains us all. Again, it is in those brief snapshot moments—and I don't mean the cute photo-op moments—when the radical risk of genuinely loving another more than ourselves comes suddenly clear.

For me, the spiritual art of negotiating the busyness of family life has been twofold. First, I have in some sense surrendered to the fact that my life is essentially one of availability. When our children were young, I felt this most intensely in the twenty-four-hour-a-day, mom-on-call experience. This availability is still the key virtue of my family life, experienced chiefly now as an unexpected midnight phone call from a distraught college-aged offspring or a family get-together orchestrated around the vision, hearing, and mobility limitations of elderly parents. However, I must make one vigorous disclaimer. Such availability must genuinely form us, not violate us. There will, no doubt, be for each of us critical times when we are stretched almost beyond our breaking points—times of serious family illness, financial distress, or unavoidable conflict. But availability does not mean being everything for everybody. It does not mean volunteering for every church, school, and civic project while you work full-time. It does not mean letting family members take undue advantage of you. Husbands can pick up their own clothes; teenagers can fix their own lunches; even small children can be taught to respect another family member's need for privacy or time alone. The availability I'm talking about is not the doormat variety; it is a more profound willingness, in things essential, to be present to others in the family, to carry their deepest interests always in your mind, to attend thoughtfully to their genuine needs, and to have the contours of your own heart stretched by the unexpected, inexplicable particularity of each of those persons you have been given to love. In this lies the beginning of our being able to love as God has loved us.

The crucial discipline to be exercised, and the one I am constantly called to practice again and again, is found in distinguishing true availability from all the demands that claim us. Americans today live in what is perhaps the most speeded up society ever to exist on earth. We are barraged by multitudinous, simultaneous instant messages about all the things we must have and must do. We overschedule our children so that they might be the best soccer, baseball, or football players, the most outstanding ballerinas, pianists, computer programmers, rocket scientists—or whatever. We overschedule ourselves so that we might have the best career, house, wardrobe, muscle tone, garden, or résumé. In our drive to have and do everything—immediately—we often seem to have forgotten that frenetic busyness is not synonymous with conscious and attentive care for each other.

The second spiritual art of a busy family life, next to genuine availability, is the art of cultivating our sense of the silence that undergirds it all. One might call this art Sabbath keeping. The idea of Sabbath keeping is, of course, embedded in the Jewish and Christian faiths. And where a family's religious observance encourages it to honor the Sabbath in traditional ways, it can be wonderful. The traditional Jewish Sabbath takes place from just before sundown Friday to just after sundown Saturday. Prohibitions from work and travel allow family relationships to become the center of focus for this most holy of days. Similarly, some Christian denominations have held Sunday (not simply the Sunday service) as a day set apart, during which faith and family are emphasized. But Sabbath keeping is not only the observance of a day. It is also about the cultivation of a certain quality of time. Sabbath time is gracious and still. It is spacious and restorative. It is not merely "time off" to refuel or run errands and is certainly not to be confused with noisy entertainment or frantic recreational activity.

Any time can be Sabbath time if it allows deep, rhythmic rest and rejuvenation to occur. Time set aside for gentle prayer or retreats, walks by the seashore, in a garden, or through the woods, quiet afternoon moments sipping a cup of tea or reading a poem before a warming fire—all these and many more moments can be Sabbath time. They honor the stillness and silence that sustain our lives. When children are young, such moments may seem elusive, but afternoon naptime might provide a window of stillness. Or a spouse arriving home from work might offer to take over for a brief time so that the other can take a summer evening walk. What is perhaps most difficult for us is resisting the habit of automatically filling time with activity or filling space with noise. We race from commitment to commitment. Radios and televisions blare while we do housework and homework. We chat on our cell phones while we drive and walk. There are, of course, occasions on which such things are necessary. But I am convinced that the conscious cultivation of Sabbath time is essential to our being able to recognize those graced snapshot moments that continually occur in the midst of our busy family lives.

I am not suggesting that we must regularly schedule Sabbath time (although this might be ideal and might, for some, be possible) but that we must consciously and intentionally honor the need for such time. However we work that out in practice is for us to decide. One family I know has a practice of setting aside Monday evenings as "goof-off" night in which all members participate. As our own children have grown, my husband and I have found ourselves on temperate Saturday or Sunday afternoons headed either north of town to Neale Woods—a nature preserve with miles of hiking trails—or out of town to some other wildlife preservation site where we soak in air and sun and the silence and stillness that drench the prairie landscapes. Sabbath time allows us to enter the busy, cluttered parts of life with perspective and some equanimity.

Family life is not only busy but it is an intensely embodied life. Bodies jostling bodies for a place at the dinner table, bodies intermingling to create new bodies, which then inhabit one and then are held, carried, nursed, tended, bathed, and fed; bodies kissed for "boo-boos"; bodies patiently accommodated as they age and fail; bodies whose proximity one longs for and whose absence inflicts pain; bodies that keep one awake by crowding into bed on a stormy childhood winter night or keep one awake long past curfew in a sultry adolescent summer; bodies that arrive unannounced for a fortnight's stay; bodies whose presence is required at holiday functions; bodies lithe and limber; bodies stiff and aching—the sacred realized in intense engagement with other bodies.

It is precisely in the fleshy encounter that those of us who marry and have children are called to experience God. God is not met in our lives solely in the solitary one-on-one encounter or in some disembodied arena clearly demarcated from the fierce, conflicting pressures of daily life. To put it in the language of Christian theology, the mystery of the incarnation itself—God becoming human—pushes us toward the insight that to encounter the infinite one must go through the finite—not around or below or above the finite—not by passing or eliminating the finite but going through it, in all its unique, unrepeatable particularity. The finite and the infinite are thus simultaneously encountered.

The startling claim of the incarnation, fully human, fully divine, becomes a lens through which all created reality can be apprehended. The finite, fleshy world is the privileged place of encounter with God.

DÍA DE LOS MUERTOS

THE DAY OF THE DEAD

Alex García-Rivera

NOVEMBER 2 IS A TIME of cemetery and church visits, home altars to the dead, special foods—including candy in the shape of skulls and skeletons—grotesque costumes, and merry dances. This festive time contrasts sharply with the subject of merriment: our inevitable rendezvous with death. What's the reason for this strange ritual?

Some say it comes from Indian roots. Others say Hispanic Catholics' love for this day stems from a tragic view of life. These explanations are probably true to some extent, but for Christians, who believe in Jesus of Nazareth, risen from the dead, there is a deeper and more satisfying explanation for this strange gladness: the Day of the Dead is a family reunion, a family fiesta.

I know what I am talking about because a young friend of mine, Estefania, has been talking to me about it for many years. You might consider this rather ordinary until I tell you that Estefania has been dead seven years. Yet Estefania has been a part of my life ever since her death. She was two months old when she died of SIDS (Sudden Infant Death Syndrome), also called crib death. Estefania's death, however, was especially tragic: she and her family were very poor.

I was with the family at the graveside ceremony. As the priest recited the familiar refrain, "Dust to dust, ashes to ashes," Estefania's father pointed to a lonely spot of ground about three feet from the grave and said, "My father is buried there." I realized we were standing on a vast plot of ground without trees or even tombstones. The significance of the place came to me: this is where they bury the poor!

I stood and wondered whether Estefania's sad burial was also a necessary prelude to some unexplained joy to come. I wondered whether her death confronted me with the reality of those who live in poverty so that I might understand their future liberation. Then I remembered the words that climaxed the funeral Mass of little Estefania, "Do this in remembrance of me." And I remembered the death and burial of Jesus, a poor man.

Frequently, the time of greatest grief in the death of a loved one occurs not at the time of death but when the casket is lowered into the grave. This is when the reality of death hits us with full force. It is the same in the gospel. Jesus had to truly die so that he could truly be raised from the dead. The reality of Jesus's death hits us with full force when his tomb is closed with a huge stone.

But Jesus's story does not end with his burial. The reality of Jesus's resurrection hits us with its full force with the image of the empty tomb. Jesus's resurrection was the act of God in defense of the son, unjustly condemned by people. God defends the innocent and does justice to those who have been treated unjustly in this life. The funeral is not the end of the story.

Estefania's funeral Mass stood in sharp contrast to the graveside ceremony. The altar linens were freshly pressed and the church was full of color and light. There was festive music and singing. Songs of resurrection filled the air and the wine sparkled in its decanter of expensive cut glass. The bread lay luxuriously on its plate of silver, ready to be served at the appropriate time of this joyful banquet. The darkness of the church was dismissed by the warm and dancing lights of candles. The procession of the priest and the acolytes with the cross was not so much a march but a dance—graceful movements with a joyful resolution.

Estefania's funeral Mass had been transformed into a Day of the Dead. The contrast of the loneliness of the cemetery stood in sharp relief to the festiveness of the Mass in the same way that the festiveness of the Day of the Dead stands in relief to its macabre subject. We had not come there, however, to laugh at death although we sang that death had lost its sting. We had not come there out of a tragic sense of life, although we repeated with the priest, "Lord, have mercy." We had come there to remember Estefania, and in remembering her, we were remembering Jesus. It is here, then, that we enter the deeper meaning of the Day of the Dead.

The crowd around Estefania's grave had been larger than any of us imagined, for, in remembering her, Mary, Saints Peter and Paul, Michael the Archangel, and all the saints had also been there with us. The community around Estefania's death was made up of the living and the dead, the past and present, that came together in joyful anticipation of an unexplained joy to come.

And thus the Day of the Dead may be a strange gladness. The Day of the Dead may be a macabre fiesta. The Day of the Dead may be a melding of Christian and pagan traditions. But if you stop there, you have missed its deeper and more profound meaning.

PRACTICING CARE FOR THE ENVIRONMENT
GOD'S STEWARDS AND CO-CREATORS

United States Conference
of Catholic Bishops

A s OTHERS HAVE POINTED OUT, we are the first generation to see our planet from space—to see so clearly
its beauty, limits, and fragility. Modern communication
technology helps us to see more clearly than ever the
impact of carelessness, ignorance, greed, neglect, and
war on the earth.

Today, humanity is at a crossroads. Having read
the signs of the times, we can either ignore the harm
we see and witness further damage, or we can take up
our responsibilities to the Creator and creation with
renewed courage and commitment.

The task set before us is unprecedented, intricate,
complex. No single solution will be adequate to the task.
To live in balance with the finite resources of the planet,

we need an unfamiliar blend of restraint and innovation. We shall be required to be genuine stewards of nature and thereby co-creators of a new human world. This will require both new attitudes and new actions.

A. New Attitudes

For believers, our faith is tested by our concern and care for creation. Within our tradition are important resources and values that can help us assess problems and shape constructive solutions. In addition to the themes we have already outlined from our social teaching, the traditional virtues of prudence, humility, and temperance are indispensable elements of a new environmental ethic. Recognition of the reality of sin and failure as well as the opportunity for forgiveness and reconciliation can help us face up to our environmental responsibilities. A new sense of the limits and risks of fallible human judgments ought to mark the decisions of policy makers as they act on complicated global issues with necessarily imperfect knowledge. Finally, as we face the challenging years ahead, we must all rely on the preeminent Christian virtues of faith, hope, and love to sustain us and direct us.

There are hopeful signs: public concern is growing; some public policy is shifting; and private behavior is beginning to change. From broader participation in recycling to negotiating international treaties, people are searching for ways to make a difference on behalf of the environment.

More people seem ready to recognize that the industrialized world's overconsumption has contributed the largest share to the degradation of the global environment. Also encouraging is the growing conviction that development is more qualitative than quantitative, that it consists more in improving the quality of life than in increasing consumption. What is now needed is the will to make the changes in public policy, as well as in lifestyle, that will be needed to arrest, reverse, and prevent environmental decay and to pursue the goal of sustainable, equitable development for all. The overarching moral issue is to achieve during the twenty-first century a just and sustainable world. From a scientific point of view, this seems possible. But the new order can only be achieved through the persevering exercise of moral responsibility on the part of individuals, voluntary organizations, governments, and transnational agencies.

In the Catholic community, as we have pointed out, there are many signs of increased discussion, awareness, and action on environment. We have offered these reflections in the hope that they will contribute to a broader dialogue in our Church and society about the moral dimensions of ecology and about the links between social justice and ecology, between environment and development. We offer these reflections not to endorse a particular policy agenda nor to step onto some current bandwagon, but to meet our responsibilities as pastors and teachers who see the terrible consequences of environmental neglect and who believe our faith calls us to help shape a creative and effective response.

B. New Actions

This statement is only a first step in fashioning an ongoing response to this challenge. We invite the Catholic community to join with us and others of good will in a continuing effort to understand and act on the moral and ethical dimensions of the environmental crisis:

• We ask scientists, environmentalists, economists, and other experts to continue to help us understand the challenges we face and the steps we need to take. Faith is not a substitute for facts; the more we know about the problems we face, the better we can respond.

• We invite teachers and educators to emphasize, in their classrooms and curricula, a love for God's creation, a respect for nature, and a commitment to practices and behavior that bring these attitudes into the daily lives of their students and themselves.

• We remind parents that they are the first and principal teachers of children. It is from parents that children will learn love of the earth and delight in nature. It is at home that they develop the habits of self-control, concern, and care that lie at the heart of environmental morality.

• We call on theologians, scripture scholars, and ethicists to help explore, deepen, and advance the insights of our Catholic tradition and its relation to the environment and other religious perspectives on these matters. We especially call upon Catholic scholars to explore the relationship between this tradition's emphasis upon the dignity of the human person and our responsibility to care for all of God's creation.

• We ask business leaders and representatives of workers to make the protection of our common environment a central concern in their activities and to collaborate for the common good and the protection of the earth. We especially encourage pastors and parish leaders to give greater attention to the extent and urgency of the environmental crisis in preaching, teaching, pastoral outreach, and action, at the parish level and through ecumenical cooperation in the local community.

• We ask the members of our Church to examine our lifestyles, behaviors, and policies—individually and institutionally—to see how we contribute to the destruction or neglect of the environment and how we might assist in its protection and restoration. We also urge celebrants and liturgy committees to incorporate themes into prayer and worship that emphasize our responsibility to protect all of God's creation and to organize prayerful celebrations of creation on feast days honoring St. Francis and St. Isidore.

• We ask environmental advocates to join us in building bridges between the quest for justice and the pursuit of peace and concern for the earth. We ask that the poor and vulnerable at home and abroad be accorded a special and urgent priority in all efforts to care for our environment.

• We urge policy makers and public officials to focus more directly on the ethical dimensions of environmental policy and on its relation to development, to seek the common good, and to resist short-term pressures in order to meet our long-term responsibility to future generations. At the very minimum, we need food and energy policies that are socially just, environmentally benign, and economically efficient.

• As citizens, each of us needs to participate in this debate over how our nation best protects our ecological heritage, limits pollution, allocates environmental costs, and plans for the future. We need to use our voices and votes to shape a nation more committed to the universal common good and an ethic of environmental solidarity.

All of us need both a spiritual and a practical vision of stewardship and co-creation that guides our choices as consumers, citizens, and workers. We need, in the now familiar phrase, to "think globally and act locally," finding the ways in our own situation to express a broader ethic of genuine solidarity.

C. Call to Conversion

The environmental crisis of our own day constitutes an exceptional call to conversion. As individuals, as institutions, as a people, we need a change of heart to save the planet for our children and generations yet unborn. So vast are the problems, so intertwined with our economy and way of life, that nothing but a wholehearted and ever more profound turning to God, the Maker of Heaven and Earth, will allow us to carry out our responsibilities as faithful stewards of God's creation.

PRACTICES *of* SPIRITUAL GROWTH

THE IGNATIAN EXAMEN

PRAYING BACKWARD
THROUGH YOUR DAY

Dennis Hamm, SJ

THE BIBLICAL PHRASE, "If today you hear his voice," implies that the divine voice must somehow be accessible in our daily experience, for this verse expresses a conviction central to Hebrew and Christian faith, that we live a life in dialogue with God. We are creatures who live one day at a time. If God wants to communicate with us, it has to happen in the course of a twenty-four-hour day, for we live in no other time. And how do we go about this kind of listening? Long tradition has provided a helpful tool, which we call the examination of consciousness today. "Rummaging for God" is an expression that suggests going through a drawer full of stuff, feeling around, looking for something that you are sure must be in there somewhere. I think that image catches some of the feel of what is classically known in church language as the prayer of "examen."

The examen, or examination, of conscience is an ancient practice in the church. In fact, even before Christianity, the Pythagoreans and the Stoics promoted a version of the practice. It is what most of us Catholics were taught to do to prepare for confession. In that form, the examen was a matter of examining one's life in terms of the Ten Commandments to see how daily behavior stacked up against those divine criteria. St. Ignatius includes it as one of the exercises in his manual, *The Spiritual Exercises.*

It is still a salutary thing to do but wears thin as a lifelong, daily practice. It is hard to motivate yourself to keep searching your experience for how you sinned. In recent decades, spiritual writers have worked with the implication that conscience in Romance languages like French (*conscience*) and Spanish (*conciencia*) means more than our English word "conscience," in the sense of moral awareness and judgment; it also means "consciousness."

Now prayer that deals with the full contents of your consciousness lets you cast your net much more broadly than prayer that limits itself to the contents of conscience, or moral awareness. A number of people—most famously, George Aschenbrenner, sj, in a classic article for *Review for Religious* in 1971—have developed this idea in profoundly practical ways. I wish to propose a way of doing the examen, as an approach in five steps:

1. *Pray for light.* Since we are not simply daydreaming or reminiscing but rather looking for some sense of how the Spirit of God is leading us, it only makes sense to pray for some illumination. The goal is not simply memory but graced understanding. That's a gift from God devoutly to be begged. "Lord, help me understand this blooming, buzzing confusion."

2. *Review the day in thanksgiving.* Note how different this is from looking immediately for your sins. Nobody likes to poke around in the memory bank to uncover smallness, weakness, lack of generosity. But everybody likes to savor beautiful gifts, and that is precisely what the past twenty-four hours contain—gifts of existence, work, relationships, food, challenges. Gratitude is the foundation of our whole relationship with God. So use whatever cues help you to walk through the day from the moment of awakening—even the dreams you recall upon awakening. Walk through the past twenty-four hours, from hour to hour, place to place, task to task, person to person, thanking the Lord for every gift you encounter.

3. *Review the feelings that surface in the replay of the day.* Our feelings, positive and negative, the painful

and the pleasing, are clear signals of where the action was during the day. Simply pay attention to any and all of those feelings as they surface, the whole range: delight, boredom, fear, anticipation, resentment, anger, peace, contentment, impatience, desire, hope, regret, shame, uncertainty, compassion, disgust, gratitude, pride, rage, doubt, confidence, admiration, shyness—whatever was there. Some of us may be hesitant to focus on feelings in this overpsychologized age, but I believe that these feelings are the liveliest index to what is happening in our lives. This leads us to the fourth moment.

4. *Choose one of those feelings (positive or negative) and pray from it.* That is, choose the remembered feeling that most caught your attention. The feeling is a sign that something important was going on. Now simply express spontaneously the prayer that surfaces as you attend to the source of the feeling—praise, petition, contrition, cry for help or healing, whatever.

5. *Look toward tomorrow.* Using your appointment calendar if that helps, face your immediate future. What feelings surface as you look at the tasks, meetings, and appointments that face you? Fear? Delighted anticipation? Self-doubt? Temptation to procrastinate? Zestful planning? Regret? Weakness? Whatever it is, turn it into prayer—for help, for healing, whatever comes

spontaneously. To round off the examen, say the Lord's Prayer. If we are to listen for the God who creates and sustains us, we need to take seriously and prayerfully the meeting between the creatures we are and all else that God holds lovingly in existence. That "interface" is the felt experience of our days. It deserves prayerful attention. It is a big part of how we know and respond to God.

SPIRITUAL DIRECTION
ACCOMPANIMENT FOR THE JOURNEY

Kathleen Fischer

S PIRITUAL DIRECTION is a conversation between a director
and someone who wants to grow in the Christian
life. Convinced that the Spirit lives in us, as well as in
all creation, the director and directee (the person being
directed) attend to God's many manifestations: Where is
God in my desire to quit my job, or in my struggle with
symptoms of Parkinson's disease? Am I being called to
take a more courageous stand on justice issues? What is
the meaning of this darkness I encounter in my prayer?

The term "direction" suggests that one person tells
another what to believe or how to act, but a spiritual
director helps others freely name what God is doing in
their lives and shape their own response. Spiritual direction is an honored practice whose roots lie deep in the
Catholic tradition. Scholars usually trace its beginnings
to the fourth-century desert fathers and mothers. In the

rugged setting of the Egyptian desert, both new and established Christians sought guidance from those considered more experienced or holy.

Throughout history, noted spiritual companions have offered diverse forms of this ministry, showing us what to look for in a spiritual friend. Teresa of Avila, for example, infused her guidance with common sense and a love of laughter. Jane Frances de Chantal reassured spiritual seekers who felt inadequate, encouraging them simply to redirect their hearts when they found themselves failing often. As practiced today, spiritual direction is especially indebted to Ignatius of Loyola, the founder of the Society of Jesus. His *Spiritual Exercises* provides not only a detailed description of the director's role (he or she should be both gentle and prudent) but also a comprehensive handbook for spiritual direction.

This ancient Christian ministry has experienced a resurgence in recent decades, its remarkable growth fueled by widespread hunger for prayer and a desire for greater intimacy with God. Though often considered a ministry of ordained clergy or vowed religious, spiritual direction embraces the gifts of the laity as well. In several of its documents, including the Dogmatic Constitution on the Church (*Lumen Gentium*), the Second Vatican Council affirmed that the vocation to holiness and ministry is universal to all the baptized. (See 33, 40.) The council's fruits can be seen in laypeople's serious attention to their spiritual lives, as well as in the growing number of laypeople serving as spiritual directors.

Who Makes a Good Spiritual Director?

Above all, we seek faith and wisdom in such a companion. But other considerations may also matter: Would you be more comfortable with a man or a woman? Why are you looking for spiritual direction at this time, and what do you hope to gain from it? Do you want an ordained minister or vowed religious, or would a married layperson better understand your life situation? How far are you willing to travel to meet with this person?

Interview two or three qualified directors. Ask about their training and experience, how they administer spiritual direction, whether they charge a fee and how it is established, how they handle confidentiality, and any other concerns you have. Notice especially how comfortable you feel with a possible director. The quality of your relationship, especially your level of trust, will be among the most important aspects of your journey, for spiritual direction entails an open and honest sharing of your story.

During your first session, you and your director will determine the basic structure for your time together, including when and how often to meet. Sessions usually last about an hour and take place once a month, but their length and frequency depend on circumstances. For instance, some individuals find having a spiritual companion during life's significant moments—retreats, important decisions, major transitions, times of illness or grief—to be enough. Since spiritual direction is a voluntary commitment, a person can stop at any time, and it is also perfectly acceptable to say that the relationship is not working. After a certain number of meetings, you and your director will usually evaluate how things are going, and mutually decide whether or not to continue.

No two spiritual direction encounters look exactly alike, for directors have unique personalities and the people they see bring a variety of experiences. However, certain elements are usually present. A session typically includes prayer, either at the beginning and end or when it arises naturally. Persons seeking direction bring what is in their hearts and on their minds: difficulties or consolations in prayer; pending decisions and significant dreams; stories of struggle or success in living the gospel. The director listens closely, sometimes mirroring back what he or she has heard or asking a question to help clarify a point. He or she may offer a suggestion, a gentle challenge, a Scripture passage, or words of encouragement.

From the earliest centuries, countless Christians have searched out seasoned guides. Whether or not we choose spiritual direction for ourselves, its ongoing popularity testifies to a perennial truth about the pilgrimage of faith: We need the love, wisdom, and witness of other travelers.

RETREATS

STEPPING BACK TO MOVE FORWARD

Anne Luther

THE CONCEPT OF A "RETREAT" has a long and varied
history. In the Christian context the invitation of
Jesus to "come away and rest awhile" (Mk. 6:31) is
often thought of as the first invitation to "make retreat."
The original inspiration for "retreat" can be traced to
the notion of a "retreat of the whole Church" in the
forty-day season of Lent as codified after the Council of
Nicaea (325) and to the development of monasticism as
a form of collective retreat.

Purpose of Retreat

The term "retreat" can be misleading in that it could
easily conjure up the idea of "escape" from the world.
The experience of "retreat" does include a "stepping
aside" from ordinary routine for a time to reflect and
to pray, to slow down, to be still, and to listen. This

"coming apart" is meant to aid retreatants in integrating their relationship with the Divine, their spirituality, as that is experienced in the marketplace and home—in the world. Ideally, the experience of retreat motivates the individual to recognize the significance of prayer, quiet, and solitude in the everyday in order to be a more "balanced" participant in every aspect of life. Spirituality concerns the whole of life and how all of life is lived in the presence of God. Retreat times, ideally, help us to wake up to the fact of the ever-present Reality in which "we live and move and have our being." Service, in the world, ought to be one of the fruits of such spiritual awakening.

Types of Retreats

In the early days of the retreat movement, the "closed retreat" would be a common phenomenon. Retreats for men only, women only, girls only, or boys only were held, consisting of conferences by a "retreat master," time for the retreatant to reflect on input, celebration of Mass, and often Benediction of the Blessed Sacrament with exposition. During some of these closed retreats, there might be an opportunity for retreatants to speak privately with the retreat master but otherwise the general order of the day was silence.

Through the years, a great variety of retreat styles has emerged. It is still common to find many retreat centers offering some form of the Spiritual Exercises of St. Ignatius in the "directed retreat experience," lasting from a short retreat of several days to the traditional four-week format. The Nineteenth Annotation retreat is also becoming more and more popular. This is a method of experiencing the Ignatian Exercises in the midst of daily life where retreatants commit themselves to a certain time of prayer each day with specific Scripture passages and then meet with a spiritual director at regular intervals, often weekly, to reflect upon what has happened in their prayer or meditation as it impacts on daily life.

Topical or thematic retreats have also become commonplace. A group of persons gather at a retreat center and spend time reflecting and praying around a specific theme such as "forgiveness," "compassion," or "the life of Jesus." Usually there is a retreat leader who offers some thoughts and reflections, passages from Scripture, or other anecdotal material touching upon the chosen theme. Retreatants are then given time and space to pray with the material they have heard. Sometimes there are opportunities for conversation among the retreatants concerning what is happening for them in this process. At other times silence is maintained throughout. This type of approach is often referred to as a "guided retreat" and usually does include some type of communal worship service depending upon the setting and the group.

Many persons opt for a "private retreat" experience where an individual retreatant takes some time for prayer, reflection, silence, and solitude at a chosen place. Many retreat centers have "hermitages" where private retreatants may stay if they choose. The hunger for a spirituality that both nourishes and challenges is being expressed everywhere by persons from a wide range of backgrounds, cultures, and religious affiliations. It is to retreat centers and houses of prayer and renewal that many of these persons go seeking a place of hospitality, safety, and peace—a place where conversations that matter may take place, where real questions may be voiced, and where some guidance is available.

LECTIO DIVINA

TRANSFORMATIVE ENGAGEMENT
WITH SCRIPTURE

Sandra M. Schneiders, IHM

A RICH PRACTICE OF BIBLICAL SPIRITUALITY or transformative engagement with the Word that is ancient but enjoying a renaissance in our own time is *lectio divina*.[1] The practice is described in the episode in Acts 8:26–39 in which the Ethiopian court official of Queen Candace is reading and meditating on the Servant Song of Isaiah (53:7–8), which he does not understand. He appeals to Philip for enlightenment. Philip's teaching results in the official's conversion and subsequent baptism.

The origin of the practice of *lectio divina* among Christians can be traced back to the desert fathers and mothers, whose spirituality consisted primarily of prayerful rumination on biblical texts. Later, in the Benedictine monasteries organized around the Rule of

St. Benedict (ca. 540), the practice was both legislated and to some extent formalized. The Carthusian Guigo II (d. ca. 1188) finally supplied a carefully articulated "method" for the practice of *lectio divina* in his spiritual classic, *Ladder of Monks*, which has been adapted by contemporary spiritual teachers for our own times.

Lectio divina is a four-step process that begins with the slow, leisurely, attentive reading (lectio) and rereading of a biblical text. Often the text is committed to memory in the process. By internalizing the text in its verbal form, one passes on to a rumination or meditation on its meaning (*meditatio*). The medieval commentaries on scripture bear witness to both the spiritual depth and the imaginative breadth to which this process could lead.

Today this second step might involve study of the text through consultation of commentaries, or reading of the text in the context of the liturgy and thus of other biblical texts from both testaments that the church sees as related, or other forms of study that open the mind to the meaning of the passage. The purpose of *meditatio* is deepened understanding of the text's meaning in the context of the person's own life and experience.

Because the text is engaged in experiential terms, the meditation gives rise to prayer (*oratio*) or response to God, who speaks in and through the text. Prayers of thanksgiving, adoration, praise, sorrow, repentance, resolve, petition, indeed all the kinds of prayer one experiences in the Psalms, are elicited as response to the Word. Finally, fervent prayer may reach that degree of interiority and union with God that the great masters of the spiritual life have called contemplation (*contemplatio*). Contemplation has acquired many meanings in the history of Christian spirituality, but in this context it indicates the full flowering of prayer in imageless and wordless union with God in the Spirit.

Lectio divina is a form of biblical spirituality in practice that, over time, can transform a person into the image of Christ encountered in scripture. I have found that many people who have never heard of *lectio divina* practice this kind of prayer on a daily basis using the New Testament, the daily lectionary, a collection of biblical texts, the Psalms, or even biblically based music. In other words, even though the term "biblical spirituality" may be unfamiliar to many people, the reality of biblical spirituality as a practice is not.

NOTE

1. A brief article on *lectio divina* with bibliography is K. W. Irwin, "Lectio Divina," in *The New Dictionary of Catholic Spirituality*, ed. M. Downey (Collegeville, Minn.: Liturgical Press, 1993), 596.

DISCERNMENT

ON CHOOSING WISELY AND WELL

David Lonsdale

O UR CHOICES ARE OUR RESPONSES to what life offers to us: taking this, accepting that; letting go of this, holding on to that; doing this rather than that; omitting or refusing to do one thing in favor of a better option. It is our choices, too, that shape our lives, and that shape reflects the kind of options we have chosen within the limits of the circumstances in which we are placed. Choices are on a sliding scale of seriousness and it goes without saying that some have greater weight than others. At one end of the scale are the more trivial decisions which we make almost automatically, without thinking, in day-to-day living. Some everyday issues, however, do have great importance: questions about how I treat my colleagues at work, whether to make sure teenagers come home on time from the movies, or how much time I spend with my community can have consequences for ourselves and others that are far reaching and far from trivial.

At the very serious end of the spectrum stand those decisions which are significant for us in that they represent truly crucial moments, turning points as a result of which our lives take a new shape and direction, are "changed utterly." It is as though at the moment of making this kind of option we gather our whole lives in our hands and, for better or worse, give them a new shape. These more crucial moments may have to do with a job, a career, a vocation, a lifestyle; a decision to marry or not to marry a particular person; a choice of celibacy; a decision to seek a divorce; a decision to ask for baptism in the church; a decision to return to the church; and so on. Most of us probably make only a few of these choices in the course of a lifetime, and spend a certain amount of time and energy running away from making them.

Christian discernment is often taken to mean only those processes of careful, prayerful deliberation which we undertake when faced with a particularly important decision. Discernment as I understand it, however, is not confined to these important moments alone. It has to do with acting in the power of the Spirit as sons and daughters of the Father and brothers and sisters of Jesus

Christ. This relationship with God—Father, Son, and Spirit—is the context in which we, as disciples of Jesus, live day by day. It is not a separate compartment of daily life, but on the contrary, the ground on which everything else stands, the fundamental relationship which roots and feeds and gives shape to life as a whole and all that it contains.

A daily, living relationship with God is a precondition for good discernment. To attempt to "do discernment" in a vacuum, as it were, by simply following a set of instructions without the foundation of this living relationship with God is a misunderstanding of what discernment is and an impossible task. It is not a mental and practical process or system which, like a book of recipes, can be taken out and used on any suitable occasion when a very important decision has to be made. This would make discernment into something automatic or mechanical, which it is not.

There are two main settings in which discernment has a place: namely, the circumstances of everyday life and, on the other hand, those occasions in which we are faced with a major decision that gives a new shape and direction to the future. Discernment in everyday life is a matter of regular reflection on daily events, within a framework of prayer, in order to see where the Spirit is leading and to follow that lead. Discernment with respect to a major decision is often a more prolonged and carefully structured process, proportionate to the seriousness of the decision itself. In each case, however, the main elements of discernment are the same. Continuing discernment in everyday life is a necessary foundation and support for discernment about major choices. If I have not practiced dancing in everyday life, I am liable to fall over on a big occasion.

The foundation of discernment in the present is recognition and awareness of the presence and action of a loving God in the past; that is, both in our personal histories and in the history of the faith community to which we belong.

Discernment also involves the practice of becoming aware of God as a day-to-day presence in our experience, not only in the past but in the present. This means recognizing the presence and action of God both in the world at large, and in the smaller, interlocking personal worlds which each of us inhabits. It requires regular prayerful reflection upon such questions as, "Where have I met God today/this week/this last month?" "Where is God meeting me and drawing me, in the events of my life and in the world around me?" "Where do I feel drawn away or cut off from God in these circumstances?"

Components of Discernment

My aim here is not to give a step-by-step description of a particular process of discernment but rather to indicate briefly the essential components of such a process.

Assiduous prayer. The climate or atmosphere necessary for good discernment is regular and serious prayer in which those involved in the process attempt to listen to the voice of the Spirit speaking in revelation and in the circumstances in which they are placed.

Adequate information. For any form of decision-making, it is imperative to have sufficient information about matters which are relevant to the choices available.

Reflection on affective responses in relation to God. This process involves noting, interpreting, and reflecting on the feelings and desires that we experience, particularly in direct or indirect response to the revelation of God.

Weighing the reasons. Being adequately informed about the circumstances surrounding each of the options available allows us to give due weight to the reasons for and against each option, which is also an essential part of the discernment process.

Confirmation. It is also to be expected that, once a decision has been made, we will experience in some form either confirmation of the decision or its opposite, unease or a sense of a need for further searching.

Christian discernment, whether in the course of daily living or in the context of a major decision, is a question of sifting through a number of different matters in turn: the circumstances and options about which choices are to be made; our feelings and thoughts about these circumstances and options within a framework of prayer and awareness of God; and the revelation of God, especially as given in the life, death, and resurrection of Jesus. In this process, we gradually become aware of harmonies or disharmonies between the mystery of Christ and our own lives, and this awareness offers a guide and norm for the choices we make.

Discernment is more than a pragmatically effective way of making choices. It is rather a framework which enables us to join in partnership with God in making choices which will help to bring about the fulfillment of God's generous hopes and desires for the world and for us.

EUCHARISTIC ADORATION

PRAYING BEFORE

Brian E. Daley, SJ

IN THE CURRENT PRACTICE of the Catholic Church in the United States, people are free to receive Communion either in the open hand or on the tongue. Although I have not conducted a survey, my impression from presiding at both student and parish liturgies is that the practice tends to vary largely along lines of age: most of the people to whom I give Communion on the tongue, at least here at Notre Dame, seem to be under 35. And while I have never attempted to find out why so many young Catholics seem to prefer this practice, I suspect it is part of a more general desire on the part of their generation to find physical, not merely verbal, ways of expressing and deepening a reverent awareness of the mystery of Christ's presence in the Eucharist.

The subject of how best to express reverence for what we Catholics so dryly call the Eucharistic "species" has become a contentious one in the church. It touches on church architecture and inner arrangement—for instance, where to place the tabernacle in which the host is reserved, and how to coordinate the placement of the tabernacle with the lectern where Scripture is read. It also includes a variety of traditional practices some would like to revive among the faithful: keeping a reverent silence in church, even outside times of liturgical celebration; genuflecting when passing in front of the tabernacle; making a profound bow before receiving Communion. Many who promote these practices feel that the liturgical changes instituted since the Second Vatican Council have unintentionally communicated to Catholics a secular spirit, in which the church building has become more a meeting place, a place for human conversation, than a sacred place where the transcendent God encounters us in human gestures and things.

One Catholic practice on which these changing sensibilities have been focused is Eucharistic adoration, a period of quiet prayer in a space primarily intended for liturgical worship—prayer focused on the sacramental bread, either reserved in a locked tabernacle or exposed to view in a monstrance. When I was growing up, this kind of devotion to the Eucharist outside the Mass was central to my developing faith, my sense of the real possibility of finding God in the life of a New Jersey parish. When Catholics in the 1950s or 1960s passed a church, it was common practice to stop in for a brief "visit" to the Lord present in the Blessed Sacrament. In that quiet place, the darkness punctuated only by a few flickering vigil lights, one had a sense that God was suddenly close, a hidden spring of life just under the surface of daily routine. Benediction of the Blessed Sacrament, a fifteen-minute service involving the exposition of the Eucharistic bread, a few familiar Latin hymns, prayers, incense, and a multitude of candles, was the normal conclusion to services other than the Mass—to novenas, vespers, and the programmatic preaching of the Catholic equivalent of a revival: the parish mission. Likewise, Holy Thursday included not only a solemn liturgy and procession, commemorating the institution of the Eucharist at Jesus's Last Supper, but also long periods of silent prayer afterward before the Sacrament itself, now moved from its normal place in the tabernacle to an altar of "repose" in some other part of the church.

Once a year, each parish celebrated the Forty Hours Devotion, too, in honor of the Blessed Sacrament—a kind of three-day community marathon of silent prayer before the exposed host, now raised high over the altar and surrounded with banks of flowers and shimmering candles. For me as a child and a teenager, these forms of Eucharistic devotion were an introduction to a peculiarly Catholic form of contemplative prayer—a prayer not so much of withdrawal from things of the senses as of kneeling and gazing, of awe-struck adoration in the midst of a throng of other worshippers. With a bit of imagination, one easily felt the words of the hymn had become real: as "all mortal flesh kept silence," the "heavenly vanguard" of angels and saints joined us in this act of ecclesial reverence. It was something richly sensual, yet pointing—through the focal point of a small white wafer—to the fullness of the church, to the heavenly liturgy, and to Jesus the eternal priest.

As in so many other aspects of Catholic life, Eucharistic devotion of this sort largely disappeared from the church's normal agenda in the late 1960s. The Eucharist, it was often pointed out, is a ritual meal, in which the whole community, gathered under the representative headship of a bishop or a priest, worships God as one body, and is nourished by the word of Scripture and the signs of Jesus's sacrifice. The purpose of the Eucharistic species, then, is not to be the object of adoration, but the daily food of God's "pilgrim people." The Second Vatican Council's Constitution on the Sacred Liturgy stated that "devotions" practiced in the church, important as they are, must be "controlled so that they cohere with the sacred liturgy, in some way derive from it, and lead the people to it" (no. 13). It also emphasized the central importance in the Mass of Scripture and the homily (no. 24), and stressed that liturgy is by its nature not a time for private prayer, but the community's public celebration (nos. 26–28). In a famous passage, the same document explicitly broadened the notion of Christ's "presence" in liturgical celebration to include not only his presence in the Eucharistic species (where he is found "most fully"—*maxime*), but also in the other sacraments, in the person of the presider, in the word of Scripture, and in the whole congregation gathered in Christ's name (no. 7).

All of this doubtless came as a needed correction of post-Reformation imbalances in the Catholic Church's life of worship. Yet it has led to some new imbalances as well: to a new emphasis on words in Catholic worship, with a corresponding de-emphasis of concrete, time-hallowed symbols; to a rationalistic barrenness in some modern church architecture and decoration; to an emphasis on community formation rather than adoration of God as the implied goal of some Sunday assemblies; to a bland moralism in a good deal of contemporary Catholic preaching; and to a tendency to self-celebration in some contemporary liturgical music. So a new reaction has been underway since at least the early 1990s, as the young seek to find contact again with the church's symbolic world and with the divine, living presence it embodies, while their elders seek to discern between healthy impulse and Baroque excess in the devotional life of the church of their youth.

In this context, Eucharistic adoration seems to be exerting a renewed attraction on young Catholics who seek to draw wisdom from the riches of the church's tradition. Renewed official guidelines for this devotion now offer a variety of forms that services of Eucharistic adoration might take, incorporating readings, a homily, and a variety of prayers, as well as quiet contemplation, hymns, and the climactic blessing of the congregation with the Eucharistic body of Christ (see "Eucharistic Worship and Devotion Outside Mass," NCCB, 1987). If used with imagination, these guidelines promise a way of reviving Eucharistic adoration within the framework of the liturgical year and the liturgical day, not as a substitute for the Mass, but as an occasion to let the heart of the Mass—our encounter with the risen Jesus in the sacramental signs of bread and wine, and in the sacramental narrative of God's saving history—become the continuing object of our thought and gaze, and invite us to deeper, more conscious participation in the Eucharistic meal.

Praying before the sacred host continues to play an important part in my own life. Although the opportunities for formal Eucharistic adoration are fewer now than when I was young, I still find the practice moving and nurturing, understated yet strangely grand. I find, too, that my routine of morning prayer, carried out in our small Jesuit community chapel in the presence of the Blessed Sacrament in the tabernacle, seems decidedly more focused, more personal, more consoling than prayer in my own room. Prayer before the Eucharist also has an inescapable churchly dimension that other forms of private prayer may lack. This is the sign, after all, around which the church gathers, to discover and nourish its authentic self as the collective body of Christ. As St. Augustine remarks in an Easter homily, "If you are the Body and the members of Christ, your own Mystery is placed on the table of the Lord—you receive your own Mystery" (Sermon 272). The attraction of Eucharistic devotion, for me at least, is that it enables us to spend time simply trying to encounter that multifaceted body as something immediate and visibly real. Prayer is always an encounter with Mystery, but it seems more obvious to me, as I pray before the Blessed Sacrament, that the Lord is there, and that in the stillness of a little room I am somehow at the heart of the church.

THE ANGELUS
TRAVELING WITH MARY
THROUGH THE DAY

Thomas H. Groome

THIS ANCIENT PRAYER PRACTICE takes its name from the Latin *angelus*, for angel, its opening word. With three Gospel verses interspersed with Hail Marys, it celebrates the Incarnation, the central tenet of Christian faith that God became human in Jesus. In this, it also highlights Jesus's mother, Mary, and her key role in God's work of salvation.

The history of the Angelus is obscure, with traces of it stretching back to ninth-century England. It seems most likely, however, that the tolling of the monastery bells calling the monks and nuns to prayer throughout the day suggested to the ordinary people that they intersperse their daily lives with prayer as well. During the sixteenth century, the tradition emerged of saying the Angelus three times a day, at six in the morning, twelve noon, and six in the evening, often prompted by the tolling of the local church bell.

℣. The angel spoke God's message to Mary,

℟. and she conceived of the Holy Spirit.

Hail, Mary . . .

℣. "I am the lowly servant of the Lord:

℟. let it be done to me according to the your word."

Hail, Mary . . .

℣. And the Word became flesh

℟. and lived among us.

Hail, Mary . . .

℣. Pray for us, holy Mother of God,

℟. that we may become worthy of the promises of Christ.

Let us pray. Loving God, fill our hearts with your grace: Once, through the message of an angel you revealed to us the incarnation of your Son; now, through his suffering and death lead us to the glory of his resurrection.

We ask this through Christ our Lord.

℟. Amen.

STATIONS OF
THE CROSS

WALKING WITH THE SUFFERING JESUS

Thomas H. Groome

FROM THE EARLIEST DAYS OF THE CHURCH, a favored devotion of Christian pilgrims to Jerusalem was to retrace the *via dolorosa*, the "path of sorrow" that Jesus walked on his journey to Calvary. St. Francis of Assisi is credited with developing the practice of replicating the Way of the Cross by an artistic depiction of its "stations"—each scene along the final journey of Jesus. You now find Stations of the Cross around the walls of most Catholic churches. Though traditionally set at fourteen, some churches have a fifteenth station representing the Resurrection. Jesus's way of the cross did not end on Calvary; God raised him up to new life for us all. One typical pattern of prayer is as follows:

- At each station, pause and say: "We adore you, O Christ, and we praise you, because by your holy cross you have redeemed the world."
- Name the station. For example, "The first station, Jesus is condemned to death."
- Mediate for a few moments on the event that the station represents.
- Pray an Our Father, Hail Mary, and Glory Be; move to the next station.

The following fourteen are the more traditional stations:

1. Jesus is condemned to death.
2. Jesus takes up his cross.
3. Jesus falls the first time.
4. Jesus meets his mother.
5. Simon of Cyrene helps Jesus to carry his cross.
6. Veronica wipes the face of Jesus.
7. Jesus falls the second time.
8. Jesus meets the women of Jerusalem.
9. Jesus falls the third time.
10. Jesus is stripped of his garments.
11. Jesus is nailed to the cross.
12. Jesus dies on the cross.
13. Jesus is taken down from the cross.
14. Jesus is laid in the tomb.

FASTING

RECLAIMING THE ANCIENT PRACTICE

Joan D. Chittister, OSB

IF IRELAND IS A BELLWETHER OF ANYTHING TODAY, it is surely of the Catholic consciousness. The Angelus still plays on public TV and radio at noon and 6 p.m. every day. "Stations"—house Masses that developed during penal times when the practice of Catholicism was forbidden by British law—are still practiced in rural areas. St. Brigid's Day is even more of a celebration in some ways than St. Patrick's Day.

But don't be deceived. All is not traditional anymore. When the waitress took our orders in a little village restaurant in the west of Ireland, for instance, she didn't know how to respond to my request that the chef wrap a starter of goat cheese in something besides ham. "The meat," I explained. "It's Lent." She looked puzzled, raised her eyebrows, and scurried away from the table, confused and embarrassed.

I was in Ireland in Lent 2006, and the Friday fast meant absolutely nothing. And why was I surprised?

The Challenge of Peace, the 1983 peace pastoral from the U.S. bishops' conference, called on Catholics to return to the Friday fast as an act of penance for peace. They wrote: "We call upon our people voluntarily to do penance on Friday by eating less food and by abstaining from meat. This return to a traditional practice of penance, once well observed in the U.S. church, should be accompanied by works of charity and service toward our neighbors. Every Friday should be a day significantly devoted to prayer, penance, and almsgiving for peace."

Almost no one I know is doing it. The question is: Should we? And if we should, why aren't we?

Fasting had a greater effect on me in my childhood than something as significant as "tran-sub-stan-ti-a-tion." Transubstantiation, they told me, was the changing of the bread and wine into the Body and Blood of Christ. But that I took for granted. Fasting, on the other hand, this foreign way of going about life, was something that called for real change in the way I lived.

In the Eucharist, Jesus changed for my sake. In fasting, I was being called to change for something far beyond my own sake. Fasting made a kind of demand on me that few other things ever did.

What it was and why anyone would do it became an even more important question as the years went by. Most of all, if the practice of fasting was so good, why had it disappeared?

When a practice strays far from its original intentions, it often must disappear so that it can be rediscovered for the right reasons. Fasting is certainly one of those practices.

I remember as a youngster dining in a convent during Lent and being curious about the small set of brass scales between every four place settings. "That's for weighing our food during Lent," the nun showing us the house explained.

Years later I entered a monastery myself. But there were no scales on the tables. The Rule of Benedict taught that we were to fast during Lent, true, but added that we were also to "add to the usual measure of our service something by way of private prayer" and "holy reading and almsgiving."

Now there was a twist. Clearly fasting was about something more than simple deprivation. Obviously fasting was supposed to add something to our lives as well as to take something away. It was meant to sensitize us to life more than it was to deprive us of it.

But when failing to fast was no longer defined as a "mortal sin," it disappeared overnight. Fasting for my generation became more burden than blessing, more an attempt to punish the body than an invitation to strengthen the soul. We managed to concentrate on beating the body down rather than showing the value of emptying ourselves of clutter so we could concentrate on something besides ourselves.

Fasting over the centuries became a kind of mathematical legerdemain of the soul. Meals had times, lengths, and quantities attached to them. The scales kept portions under four ounces; the distinction between juices and soups and solids kept us paranoid about the differences between them. If heaven and hell depend on it, a person can get very nervous. No wonder modern psychology found fasting suspect. It had lost all semblance of sense for the heart or gift for the soul.

When Vatican II came along with its emphasis more on spirit than rules, people put down some rules immediately. Fasting, for obvious reasons, was one of them.

But the practice of fasting cannot be easily dismissed. Fasting is the unfinished chapter in post–Vatican II spirituality because the reasons for it abound.

The place of fasting in the lives of all the great spiritual figures in history brings no small amount of weight to the subject. Time, too, recommends we revisit the subject, as fasting has been a constant tradition in the church for twenty centuries. Finally, the presence of fasting in all spiritual traditions, not just Catholicism, makes a person pause. In all places and times, fasting has been a hallmark of the person on a serious search for the spiritual dimensions of life.

How do we explain the meaning of fasting in our time? The answers ring with the kind of simplicity and depth common only to the holiest of disciplines. The fact is that the values of fasting strike to the heart of a person, sharpen the soul to the presence of God, and energize the spirit in a way engorgement never can.

Fasting calls a person to authenticity. It empties us, literally, of all the nonessentials in our lives so we have room for God. It lifts our spirits beyond the mundane.

Fasting confronts our consumer mentality with a reminder of what it is to be dependent on God. It reminds us that we are not here simply to pamper ourselves. We are, indeed, expected to be our brother and sister's keeper. We know why we are hungry. We voluntarily gave up the food we could have had. But why are they hungry? Where is the food they should be eating? And what can we do to fill them now that we are done filling only ourselves?

Fasting opens us to the truth. It makes space in us to hear others, to ask the right questions, to ingest the answers we have been too comfortable to care about for far too long. It makes room for adding "to our service a bit more prayer and reading and almsgiving," as the Rule of Benedict says.

Fasting requires us to develop a sense of limits. No, we may not have it all, do it all, and demand it all. Our needs do not exceed the needs of others, and our needs may never become more important than theirs.

Fasting teaches us to say no to ourselves in small things so that we may have the strength to say no to those people and systems and governments who want to use us to shore up their own power and profit despite the needs of others.

When we fast, we become voluntarily poor and so understand the needs of the poor.

When we fast, we say yes to the Spirit and no to the lusts within us that drive us to live for money and power and profit and the kind of engorgement that renders the rest of the world destitute.

No doubt about it: Fasting surely has something to do with peacemaking. It puts us in touch with the Creator. It puts us in touch with ourselves. It puts us in touch with the prophet Jesus who, fasting in the desert, gave up power, wealth, comfort, and self-centeredness, and teaches us to do the same. It puts us in touch with the rest of the creation whose needs now cry out in our own.

THANKSGIVING AFTER COMMUNION

HEART TO HEART WITH JESUS

Thomas H. Groome

A T THE TIME of my First Holy Communion, I learned a pattern to follow in making a thanksgiving. It's a little mnemonic that prompts the sentiments that one might express to Jesus. Amazingly, for almost sixty years now I've followed it every time I receive Eucharist. I don't think it was my Mom who taught me, so it must have been Miss Geraghty, my second-grade teacher.

It is easy to remember—around the word ALTAR. So, as a thanksgiving after receiving Communion, and with a view to bringing our lives to the Eucharist and the Eucharist to our lives, we might express these sentiments.

- *Adoration*: pause to be in awe and amazement at this moment of divine/human encounter; welcome Jesus and thank him for coming to you in the Eucharist;

- *Love*: tell Jesus you love him and ask him to kindle the same spark of love in your heart for others that is so aflame in his for us all;

- *Talk*: talk to Jesus about your life, about what you're "up to" and whatever is "going on" there; review your joys and sorrows, hopes and concerns with Jesus;

- *Ask*: recognize the help and blessings you need in your life at this time and ask Jesus for the graces of which you are most in need;

- *Repent/Resolve*: ask forgiveness as needed and make resolutions about how you will try to live as a disciple of Jesus, placing your life in his hands.

SPIRITUAL PRACTICE GOES DIGITAL

FAITH RESOURCES ONLINE

Barbara Radtke

CAN MY IPAD HELP ME PRAY? Can Twitter be a vehicle for sharing my faith with friends? Can Facebook help me express my authentic spiritual self? In the information age, it may seem counterintuitive to expect digital technology to assist practitioners with their spiritual activities. With digital devices always at our fingertips, our first thought may be that digital technology is nothing but a distraction from spiritual practice. Our instinct may be to unplug if and when we want to "be spiritual."

Yet digital media can and does play a role in supporting and sustaining spiritual activity. In "Faith Online," the Pew Internet and American Life Project's study published in 2004, we learn that almost two-thirds of those who had access to the Internet, about eighty-two million Americans, have used it for spiritual or religious reasons.[1] This online activity did not replace a faith community but was used mostly in addition to affiliation with a congregation. Do not be fooled into thinking that this demographic is strongly biased toward youth. In a more recent Pew Study, "Generations 2010," Kathryn Zickuhr demonstrates that searching for information about religion on the Internet is more popular as the demographic gets older.[2] However, age does make a difference in the type of devices that people use to access the information. In a 2011 address, Kristen Purcell observed that young adults are the leading group to use mobile devices to access the Internet.[3]

Looking specifically at Catholic spirituality in practice, digital media is used in three ways: (1) to introduce and inform people about a practice and its history, (2) to connect people who are interested in a practice so they can relate experiences and exchange resources, and (3) to renew a practice in a new medium or to model the practice.

An introduction to and information about a practice may be the most well-known way the Internet has been used. Going back to the 2004 Pew study, almost a quarter of the respondents had used the Internet to gather information about the celebration of religious holidays or to find out where they could connect with religious services. A parish that places its weekly bulletin online may provide such information. Identifying favorite "go-to" sites is helpful for easy access. You can bookmark parish and diocesan sites and the site of the U.S. Catholic bishops (http://www.usccb.org) and be confident of the information provided. Many Catholic publishing houses provide informative articles to bring people to their websites. The Franciscan St. Anthony's Press (http://www.americancatholic.org), for example, offers abundant free resources and archives a number of its publications. *Catholic Update*, which comes out monthly, is a popular source on many Catholic themes including spiritual practices. The authors are often well known, and additionally, each *Update* issue has an imprimatur. Loyola Press (http://www.loyolapress.com) has a number of useful blogs and interactive tools to engage readers. You can log on to the Loyola site for their three-minute retreat or their daily inspiration features. A popular site for young adults in their twenties and thirties to gather information about Catholic practices is http://bustedhalo.com. Key to using the Internet for information is knowing one can trust the site consulted. If the site is not a known entity, one can consult any

university library website to find criteria for evaluating
a website.

When people use the Internet so they can connect
with others or share their own experiences, they are
using the social networking aspects of the World Wide
Web. A tool such as Facebook provides an interactive
way to share faith. For example, at this writing, the
author Fr. James Martin, sj, uses this tool to share spiritual thoughts daily. He maintains an ongoing dialogue
with his readers, who often reply to his posts. It is not
necessary to be a published author to practice sharing
spiritual insights regularly. A friend who is a physician,
after a day with patients in his practice, regularly posts
a spiritual thought for the day on Facebook. He is well
known for this service among his friends and family, who
look for his message and often write a small response to
his post. Twitter is another popular vehicle for this kind
of sharing.

There are possibilities for deeper reflection and more
sustained conversation in discussion forums through
password-protected sites. Several universities, including Boston College's C21 Online program (http://bc.edu
/c21online), offer noncredit possibilities for people
to focus on faith formation and spiritual renewal.
Different organizations for ministry have teamed up

with publishing houses to provide other online events. While some of these opportunities are structured as a course with moderated discussion, others are designed like webinars or conferences. In most of these experiences, people not only discover resources but also have an opportunity to interact.

In the third way of using the Internet, someone models a practice in this new media. One might think that the Internet is an unfriendly medium for conveying the potential of prayer and retreat, but a look at a few select sites will dispel such a notion. The site of artist Bob Gilroy, SJ (http://www.prayerwindows.com), offers ways to pray with original art and structures a way to take an online retreat. Gilroy provides an idea that could easily be extended. With the availability of works of art online and one of the many slideshow tools available online, it is easy to make a gallery of images that can provide a moment for meditation or prayer. Like the prayer cards with depictions of Jesus, Mary, and the saints, our smartphones and other mobile devices as well as our computers become means to occasion prayer. The Irish Jesuits (http://www.sacredspace.ie) suggest ways to use their site for daily prayer and offer guidance on different forms of prayer. The British Jesuits (http://www.pray-as-you-go.org) offer downloadable daily prayer experiences with music and questions for reflection based on the lectionary reading. They even deliver the daily reading to one's social media account.

Users of digital media have found creative ways to use digital technology. At an appointed time, a friend of mine who is a sister in a vowed religious community turns on her iPad and uses the FaceTime application to contact a sister in her community who lives in another state. (They could just as easily use Skype on their computer instead.) Through FaceTime, they can see and hear each other seated in their living rooms. They greet each other and then they pray part of the Liturgy of the Hours together. For my friend, praying with members of her community this way is a tremendous support because she does not live in close proximity to anyone in her community.

In his forty-fifth World Communication Day address, on January 24, 2011, Pope Benedict XVI called the Web a contribution to "the development of new and more complex intellectual and spiritual horizons, new forms of shared awareness." Enriching, deepening, and renewing our spiritual life is an ongoing journey. Digital technology may help pave your route.

NOTES

1. Lynn Clark et al., "Faith Online," April 7, 2004, http://www
   .pewinternet.org/PPF/r/126/report_display.asp.

2. Kathryn Zickuhr, "Generations 2010," December 16, 2010,
   http://pewinternet.org/Reports/2010/Generations-2010
   /Overview.aspx.

3. Kristen Purcell, "Trends to Watch: News and Information
   Consumption," March 24, 2011, the Catholic Press
   Association, http://pewinternet.org/Presentations/2011/Mar
   /Catholic-Press-Association.aspx.

KEEP ON PRACTICING

YOU'LL GET BETTER AT IT

Thomas H. Groome

THE YOUNG MUSICIAN from Ohio was mesmerized by New York City and very excited about her upcoming audition. As she emerged from the subway at the corner of Fifty-Sixth and Seventh, however, she felt disoriented. She knew her destination was around here somewhere, but in which direction? Then, to her relief, she saw an elderly man coming toward her, with a violin case tucked under his arm. *Ah, he must surely know,* so she inquired, "Excuse me sir, can you tell me how to get to Carnegie Hall?" The old musician halted, looked pensive for a moment, and then offered, "Practice, practice, practice." We can say the same about Catholic Christian faith; being any good at it requires lots of practice.

The Reformation era was occupied with an intense debate about the nature of Christian faith. A great battle cry of the Reformers was that "faith alone" by "grace alone" brings salvation, granting little significance to people's own efforts and "good works." When the Catholic Church regathered at the Council of Trent (1545–63), it granted that we are saved by faith—which is always a gift of God—but this faith must be lived in every day of life. And even though we live as Christians only with the help of God's grace, we are still held responsible for making our own best efforts. In sum, Trent insisted that "faith without works is dead" (Jas. 2:17), that good works are integral to the Christian life. We literally *must* practice our faith.

The daily practice of Christian faith, of course, cannot be reduced to saying prayers or doing spiritual exercises. The core Christian practices are to live the great commandment of love, to embrace the spirit of the Beatitudes, to do the works of mercy and compassion, to work for justice and peace in the world. In sum, our practice of Christian faith should help to realize the reign of God. We cannot simply pray for its coming, as in "thy kingdom come"; we must also do God's will "on earth," that is, in daily life, "as it is done in heaven." This is what it means to live as a disciple of Jesus.

This emphasis on practicing the faith, living as disciples, lends a particular distinction to Catholic spirituality. Far more than simply saying prayers or doing pious things, Catholic spirituality requires people to consciously put their faith to work in the ordinary and the everyday of lives. Catholic spirituality means that Christian faith should permeate and direct our every "thought, word, and deed"—as the old Morning Offering put it.

This being said—that Christians are to live their faith through their whole way of being in the world—we then recognize that good habits of prayer and spiritual practices can help to inspire, guide, and sustain such lived faith in the day-to-day. Prayer practices both heighten our God-consciousness about life and lend us access to God's grace in Jesus that St. Paul says we need for doing "an abundance of every good work" (2 Cor. 6:8). In other words, we need practices of prayer and spirituality to nurture and sustain our efforts, which we mount by God's grace, to live lives of Christian faith.

For example, a good morning offering can surely help orient one's day toward living as a disciple of Jesus. It sharpens a person's God-consciousness to permeate every aspect of the day that follows. If you don't like the traditional one we've offered here, make up your own. I did so about thirty years ago and have used it ever since. I call it my "foundation prayer" because it helps me to begin each day with a review of my groundings in faith, while asking God for the graces I need to live them. Likewise, to do an "examen" at day's end helps us recognize whether we responded well or poorly to the movements of God's Spirit this day, inspiring our efforts for tomorrow.

Besides helping to sustain and deepen lives in faith, consistent spiritual practices are key, as social scientists now assure us (as any parent could intuit), to forming children and youth in Christian identity. In sum, the most likely way to raise Christians is to have them do Christian things. Young people need to become well informed in the beliefs of Christian faith, but more formative by far are regular faith practices. It's practices more than theory that make Christians.

In this slim volume, we've offered only a sample from the rich treasury of Catholic spirituality. You'll find dozens more practices of prayer, care, and growth within every instance of ethnic Catholicism. Hispanic cultures, for example, brim with popular spiritual practices; we touched on only two here (*Las Posadas* and Día de los Muertos). Much the same can be said of the Polish, Italian, Irish, and so on. And if you don't like the ones here or what you find in your tradition, make up your own. I know a single mother who performs a brief nightly ritual with her three young children. She simply takes each child in her arms at bedtime, gives them a hug, and says, "God loves you and so do I." I'll wager that those children will grow up knowing deeply that they are loved by God, as well as by their mom. What a great foundation for a life lived in faith.

The old adage that "practice makes perfect" is likely not true in the spiritual life; we never quite reach perfection. Even the greatest saints recognized their shortcomings. However, Jesus did say, "be holy as your heavenly Father is holy" (Matt. 5:48). What a high standard! It surely means that the journey into fullness of faith is lifelong; we cannot rest until we finally rest in God. In the meantime, good prayer practices and spiritual exercises will help to sustain our reach toward fullness of faith, to approximate the holiness of God. If we keep on practicing, we'll surely get better at it.

PERMISSIONS AND ACKNOWLEDGMENTS

"Catholic Spirituality in Practice" by Colleen M. Griffith was rewritten for this volume.

"The Lord's Prayer" by N. T. Wright is excerpted from *The New Westminster Dictionary of Christian Spirituality*, ed. Philip Sheldrake, Westminster John Knox Press. Used with permission. All rights reserved.

"Praying with the Saints" by Elizabeth A. Johnson is excerpted from *Friends of God and Prophets: A Feminist Theological Reading of the Communion of Saints*, © 1999. Reprinted with the permission of the publisher, The Continuum International Publishing Group.

"The Jesus Prayer" by Joseph Wong is excerpted from *Religion East and West*, Issue 5. Used with permission. All rights reserved.

"Intercessory Prayer" by Ann Ulanov and Barry Ulanov is excerpted from *Primary Speech: A Psychology of Prayer*, Westminster John Knox Press. Used with permission. All rights reserved.

"Centering Prayer" by Joseph G. Sandman is reprinted with permission of America Press, Inc. © 2000. All rights

ABOUT THE CONTRIBUTORS

Joan Chittister, osb, former prioress of the Benedictine sisters of Erie, is a weekly columnist for the *National Catholic Reporter*.

Elizabeth Collier is Visiting Assistant Professor of Religious Studies at DePaul University in Chicago.

Brian E. Daley, sj, is the Catherine F. Huisking Professor of Theology at the University of Notre Dame and specializes in early Christian theology.

Esther de Waal is a married laywoman and a distinguished scholar of Celtic spirituality. Since she wrote this article, Esther de Waal has followed up this theme in her writings, notably *The Celtic Way of Prayer* (Doubleday, 1996) and *Lost in Wonder: Rediscovering the Spiritual Art of Attentiveness* (Liturgical Press, 2003).

Kathleen Fischer is a counselor, spiritual director, and widely published author.

Alejandro (Alex) García-Rivera (1951–2010) was a pioneering theologian who was originally trained in physics, but his scholarship bridged the disciplines of science, art, and religion.

COLLEEN M. GRIFFITH is associate professor of the practice of theology and faculty director of spirituality studies in the Department of Religious Education and Pastoral Ministry at Boston College's School of Theology and Ministry.

THOMAS H. GROOME is professor of theology and religious education at Boston College, and chair of the Department of Religious Education and Pastoral Ministry at Boston College's School of Theology and Ministry.

DENNIS HAMM, SJ, a Scripture scholar, holds the Graff Chair in Catholic Theology at Creighton University, Omaha, Nebraska.

ELIZABETH A. JOHNSON, CSJ, is Distinguished Professor of Theology at Fordham University.

DAVID LONSDALE teaches Christian spirituality and pastoral theology at Heythrop College, University of London, where he is senior lecturer and dean of postgraduate studies.

ANNE LUTHER is director of Adult Spiritual Renewal & Empowerment, Inc., and serves as adjunct faculty at the Institute of Pastoral Studies at Loyola University, Chicago.

Ana María Pineda is associate professor of religious studies at Santa Clara University, California.

Barbara Radtke is instructional designer for continuing education at Boston College's School of Theology and Ministry.

Joseph G. Sandman vice president for university advancement at Seton Hall University, was formerly vice president at Xavier University (Cincinnati) and Loyola University in Chicago.

Sandra M. Schneiders, ihm, is professor of New Testament studies and Christian spirituality at the Jesuit School of Theology/Graduate Theological Union.

Marjorie J. Thompson is director of Pathways in Congregational Spirituality/Director, Companions in Christ, Nashville, Tennessee.

Ann Ulanov is professor of psychiatry and religion at Union Theological Seminary. The late Barry Ulanov was professor of English emeritus at Barnard College, Columbia University. Together, they authored works on religion, spirituality, and prayer.

THE UNITED STATES CONFERENCE OF CATHOLIC BISHOPS (USCCB) is an assembly of the hierarchy of the United States and the U.S. Virgin Islands who jointly exercise certain pastoral functions on behalf of the Christian faithful of the United States.

JOSEPH WONG, OSB, CAM, is a member of the Camaldolese Benedictines and resides in Camaldoli, Italy.

N. T. WRIGHT was, until 2010, bishop of Durham. He is now Research Professor of New Testament and Early Christianity at the University of St. Andrews in Scotland.

WENDY M. WRIGHT is professor of theology at Creighton University and holds the John C. Kenefick Faculty Chair in the Humanities.

the CHURCH | *in the* 21ST CENTURY CENTER

The Church in the 21st Century Center at Boston College offers dynamic programming, publications, and web and digital media materials to be a catalyst and resource for the renewal of the Catholic Church. www.bc.edu/church21

About Paraclete Press

Who We Are

Paraclete Press is a publisher of books, recordings, and DVDs on Christian spirituality. Our publishing represents a full expression of Christian belief and practice—from Catholic to Evangelical, from Protestant to Orthodox.

We are the publishing arm of the Community of Jesus, an ecumenical monastic community in the Benedictine tradition. As such, we are uniquely positioned in the marketplace without connection to a large corporation and with informal relationships to many branches and denominations of faith.

What We Are Doing

BOOKS | Paraclete publishes books that show the richness and depth of what it means to be Christian. Although Benedictine spirituality is at the heart of all that we do, we publish books that reflect the Christian experience across many cultures, time periods, and houses of worship. We publish books that nourish the vibrant life of the church and its people—books about spiritual practice, formation, history, ideas, and customs.

We have several different series, including the best-selling Paraclete Essentials and Paraclete Giants series of classic texts in contemporary English; A Voice from the Monastery—men and women monastics writing about living a spiritual life today; award-winning poetry; best-selling gift books for children on the occasions of baptism and first communion; and the Active Prayer Series that brings creativity and liveliness to any life of prayer.

RECORDINGS | From Gregorian chant to contemporary American choral works, our music recordings celebrate sacred choral music through the centuries. Paraclete distributes the recordings of the internationally acclaimed choir Gloriæ Dei Cantores, praised for their "rapt and fathomless spiritual intensity" by *American Record Guide,* and the Gloriæ Dei Cantores Schola, which specializes in the study and performance of Gregorian chant. Paraclete is also the exclusive North American distributor of the recordings of the Monastic Choir of St. Peter's Abbey in Solesmes, France, long considered to be a leading authority on Gregorian chant.

VIDEOS | Our videos offer spiritual help, healing, and biblical guidance for life issues: grief and loss, marriage, forgiveness, anger management, facing death, and spiritual formation.

Learn more about us at our website: www.paracletepress.com, or call us toll-free at 1-800-451-5006.

SCAN TO READ MORE

ALSO AVAILABLE

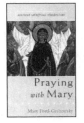

Praying with Mary
Mary Ford-Grabowsky

80 pages
ISBN: 978-1-61261-137-2
$24.95 (pack of 5), Small paperback

Praying the Holy Scriptures
M. Basil Pennington, OCSO

64 pages
ISBN: 978-1-61261-141-9
$24.95 (pack of 5), Small paperback

Praying with Icons
Linette Martin

64 pages
ISBN: 978-1-61261-058-0
$24.95 (pack of 5), Small paperback

Praying the Jesus Prayer
Frederica Mathewes-Green

64 pages
ISBN: 978-1-61261-059-7
$24.95 (pack of 5), Small paperback

Available from most booksellers or
through Paraclete Press:
www.paracletepress.com
1-800-451-5006